Flies in the Face of Fashion,

Mites Make Right,

and Other Bugdacious Tales

Flies in the Face of Fashion,
Mites Make Right,
and Other Bugdacious Tales

by Tom Turpin

Purdue University Press
West Lafayette, Indiana

Printed in the United States of America.

ISBN 978-1-55753-417-0
      1-55753-417-9

Library of Congress Cataloging-in-Publication Data

Turpin, Tom, 1943-
  Flies in the face of fashion, mites make right, and other
bugdacious tales / by Tom Turpin.
      p. cm.
  Includes bibliographical references (p.   ) and index.
   ISBN-13: 978-1-55753-417-0 (alk. paper)
   ISBN-10: 1-55753-417-9
   1. Insects. I. Title.
   QL463.T87 2006
   595.7--dc22

                                    2006001190

CONTENTS

Introduction

They're everywhere! Worldwide there are around one million species of insects and many more yet to be discovered. For each pound of human tissue on the earth, it has been estimated that there are seventy pounds of insects. It would be impossible for any human being to live a normal life on this earth without encounters of the insect kind.

So what, exactly, are these critters? Insects are a type of animal called an invertebrate—an animal that has no backbone. Insects belong to the phylum of arthropods, which also includes spiders, ticks, millipedes, centipedes, sowbugs, lobsters, crayfish, and shrimp. All of these creatures have an exoskeleton. Insects form a special class of animals within this group that have certain features in common: six legs; a body that is divided into three obvious sections, the head, thorax, and abdomen; and two antennae.

Long before reality TV popularized competition between groups of organisms, a confrontation of epic proportions was unfolding on the third rock from the sun. It was the battle between insects and humans. A biological war for dominion of the earth had begun. The conflict continues unabated to this day.

The insects had a head start. If possession is 90 percent of the law, this war has been an uphill battle for humans. The creatures that are similar to what today we call insects first appeared on the earth about 350 million years ago. Humans, by comparison, have been around for less than a million years. If time is money, team insect had banked a lot of investment capital in

terms of survival skills by the time team human entered the fray for biological supremacy of the planet.

Very few people would deny that humans and insects are two of the most successful types of animals on the earth. Humans can credit much of their success to their large brain and an opposing thumb on a digit-endowed limb. As a result humans are problem solvers and construct tools to do things beyond their physical capabilities—for instance, airplanes for air travel. Insects don't reason, nor do they have hands, but they have come to occupy almost every nook and cranny of nature.

The phenomenal success of insects is due to several biological attributes. Their small size means that individuals do not need a lot of food and can live in small spaces. The smallest are about $1/_{100}$ of an inch in length, small enough to pass through the eye of a needle.

Many insects can fly in the adult stage. Some maintain sustained flight of over 30 miles per hour. They use flight to find food, shelter, and mates. In addition, the ability to fly allows insects to avoid predators and offers a way to move to new areas.

Insects, and a few other animals, such as frogs, toads, and salamanders, metamorphose. That is, these animals have two distinctly different forms during their life: the immature and the adult stages. The different stages live in different habitats and do not compete with each other for food and space. For instance, immature Japanese beetles are called grubs and feed on plant roots. Adult Japanese beetles fly above ground and feed on leaves and flowers.

Insects, like their biological relatives the spiders and crayfish, possess an exoskeleton. The exoskeleton combines the functions of the human skeleton and skin. Very much like a suit of armor, the exoskeleton is tough and strong. But having an exoskeleton means that it has to be shed, a process known as

molting, for the insect to grow. But the advantages of protection provided by the exoskeleton exceed the disadvantages of a periodical need to molt.

Insects also exhibit what is known in biology as a high reproductive rate. Many female insects produce over a hundred eggs during their lifetime. But queens of some social insects can produce hundreds of thousands of eggs during their lives. In the twenty-first century—that's human, not insect, time—the battle for control of the earth hangs in the balance. The most modern technology cannot entirely keep insects from doing things we do not like. Insects still transmit human diseases, destroy our belongings, and attack our animals. But they are still playing the important ecological roles that they have for millions of years. Roles like pollination, destruction of dead plant and animal material, and food for other animals. It is unlikely that humans will ever have dominion over the insects. After all, as British geneticist and evolutionary biologist J. B. S. Haldane was purported to have said: "The Creator, if he exists, had an inordinate fondness for beetles." And, I might add, insects in general!

Enlightenment?

Insects & Humans

Humans don't get along well with insects. At least a high percentage of people express a disdain for insects. In response to surveys about feelings for insects 50% of people say they are apprehensive, 20% say they are fearful, and 5% report they are phobic. Twenty percent of humans indicate that they are indifferent to insects while only 5% say they like insects. If this were a political poll the approval rating for insects is only 5% while 75% disapprove of these creatures.

There are lots of reasons to disapprove of insects. These six-legged creatures damage our plants, our possessions, and bite and sting our animals and us. Insect-borne diseases have been responsible for untold numbers of human deaths through the ages. And insects just plain annoy us.

Insects and the diseases they carry have had a dramatic influence on the history of the world. Fleas vectored the plague, a disease that contributed to the downfall of the feudal system of Medieval England. Mosquitoes are vectors for a number of diseases. Mosquito-borne yellow fever resulted in the failure of the French to build the Panama Canal. The United States was able to manage the mosquito problem and subsequently completed construction of the canal.

Malaria, also transmitted by mosquitoes, is said to have contributed to the decline of the great ancient civilizations of Rome and Greece. Malaria is essentially a disease of the tropics and subtropics. Today 41 percent of the world's population live in malaria-infested areas, and estimates of deaths due to this disease range from 700,000–2.7 million per year. The protozoa that

causes malaria and the *Anopheles* mosquitoes that vector it were introduced into North America on slave ships. As a result for many years the area around the Great Lakes was one of the highest malaria areas in the world. In the United States, malaria has been eradicated since the 1950s.

Mosquitoes also vector West Nile Virus. Body lice are responsible for transmitting typhus. The tse tse fly carries sleeping sickness. House flies can transfer organisms that cause typhoid, dysentery, or cholera. The conenose bug transmits Chagas' disease. The bed bug doesn't transmit any diseases, but it does take a blood meal from humans when it gets the chance.

From a medical standpoint there are lots of justifiable reasons to hate insects. In fact Carl Sagan in *Dragons of Eden* suggested that a fear of insects might have contributed to our survival in the early days of humankind. Encoded in our genes, that survival mechanism is expressed today in our fear of the only remaining dragons "the insects."

Insects are sometimes called the "the good, the bad, and the ugly" for good reason. The good side is probably the most poorly understood aspect of the insect world. These creatures are essential to the ecological stability of the earth. Without insects there would be no showy flowers. Flowers exist to attract insect pollinators. Many animals would not exist because they depend on insects as a food resource. Insects are also important recyclers for organic material. Dead animals and dead plants are fed upon by a number of insect species. Insects also play important ecological roles by consuming live plant and animal tissue.

And lest we forget, insects are also important as inspiration for our art and literature. We find insects in poetry, novels, songs, art renderings, dance, plays, songs and in folklore.

So What's Bugging You?

Little boys have been known to "bug" older sisters and sometimes parents. Operatives of secret organizations fear "bugged" meeting rooms. Gossips have sometimes put a "bug" in a willing listener's ear. And we have all slept "snug as a bug in a rug" on a cold winter's night.

The word "bug" conjures up all kinds of ideas in people's minds. For instance, mentally ill people are sometimes incarcerated in a "bug house," and society has come to regard such folks as "buggy." Most of us have at some time in our lives committed a bug-a-boo, to the dismay of our colleagues. But what do children look like when they are "cute as a bug's ear"?

We may never know the answer to that question, since bugs don't have real ears, but most of our current uses of the word "bug" reflect an ancient meaning similar to the Celtic word "bwg" (pronounced BOOG), which meant ghost or spirit. Such an idea, and the word, is incorporated into the thought of the boogey man—that mystical spirit of darkness sometimes used by parents to keep children in line.

The word "bwg" was probably first used to describe the bed bug. This pest of humans is rather reclusive in its habits. It hides in cracks and crevices of houses during the day. It emerges at night and, under the cover of darkness, attacks sleeping humans. To the ancient Celts who fell victim to this insect, it must surely have seemed that they were victims of a ghost or spirit. Thus, the name bwg. We call the shy creature a bed bug and, to this day, admonish, "Good night, sleep tight, and don't let the bed bugs bite."

Scientifically, "bug" is used to describe members of the insect order Hemiptera, the true bugs of the insect world. Bugs include such aquatic insects as the giant water bug, water striders, and backswimmers. And on our plants, we sometimes find squash bugs, stink bugs, and boxelder bugs. Ambush bugs and assassin bugs are, as their names suggest, predators—mostly on other insects. Kissing bugs, like the bed bugs, are pests of humans. They get their name from the habit of biting folks around the mouth.

Regardless of its scientific merit, the word "bug" is frequently used in reference to any insect. An entomological error! You see, all bugs are insects, but not all insects are bugs.

Such a mistake was made by the computer folks who discovered that an insect had short-circuited their computer. The insect was a moth—not a bug—but after its removal, they coined the term "debug" to describe the process of fixing a nonfunctioning computer.

Oh well, most entomologists don't worry about the misuse of the term "bug." You see, like a lot of other folks, we have learned not to let the little things in life bug us.

Take Two Maggots and Call Me in the Morning

Insects play a major role in human health. These six-legged creatures cause us health problems because of direct feeding or transmission of disease-causing organisms.

But on the other hand, a few insects and their products have been used by humans to improve health. One example is the ancient technique of using biting insects to suture a wound. Ants and beetles are good for this since they have well-developed mandibles. Many primitive people throughout the world still use this procedure for wounds.

How does insect suturing work? First, you catch the insect and induce it to spread out its jaws. When the jaws of the insect are open, pinch the skin together and let the insect clamp down on the folds. Once the jaws are clamped in place, the head of the insect is pinched off. The head, with the jaws, remains in place and provides a suture. This technique is very much like the metal staples that modern surgeons use as sutures.

For symptoms of a cold, such as stuffiness, phlegm accumulation, and headache, try what the Australian aborigines do. They make a liquid concoction out of green tree ants. A swig or two of this mixture is believed to provide relief from the miseries of a cold.

Honey bees also provide some help with human health. For instance, honey has been used for thousands of years as a dressing for wounds. The sugar content and the acidity of honey reduce the risk of harmful microorganisms growing and causing infections.

11

Many people like to consume locally produced honey to help develop a tolerance to local pollen. This is said to help people who suffer from hay fever during the plant growing season.

The venom in the honey bee's sting has been purported to provide relief from the pain of arthritis. Some people go so far as to induce bees to sting arthritic joints in an effort to reduce the pain. It might be that the pain of the sting overrides the pain of arthritic joints! Whatever the reason, some people swear by the treatment.

One of the most interesting uses of bees or their products for health purposes is associated with royal jelly. This substance is produced by the glands of worker bees and is fed to newly hatched larvae. Larvae destined to become queens receive the substance all through their immature lives.

Everyone knows how vigorous honey bee queens are. So it is probably not a surprise that the substance so important to their development has been used to cure all sorts of ailments.

According to the printed material associated with Peking Royal Jelly, each 10 cc vial contains 250 mg of royal jelly mixed in with a couple of herbs. It helps cure loss of body weight and weakness after illness or childbirth. It also helps overcome general weakness in mental and physical energy and overtaxation. Got a chronic disease of the liver or anemia or a gastric ulcer? Royal jelly will help. No, it really won't.

The most interesting of all insect-related cures is called maggot therapy. It's the use of maggots to help heal wounds and sores. It works like this. Maggots are introduced into the wound. The maggots eat the decaying flesh while their waste material helps inhibit infection. Maggot therapy has been used for almost four centuries.

Colonies of flies are still maintained in some hospitals for use in maggot

therapy. But the substance that helps wounds heal, called allantoin, has been commercially produced. It seems some people are a bit squeamish about having live maggots crawl around in their wounds. I guess you could say that the idea just bugs them!

Scientist studying ancient fossils have dated insect remains as far back as 380 million years old, but estimate that insects have been on earth since 450 million years ago. That's way older than dinosaurs, who came around 250 million B.C. Insects have been found trapped in chunks of amber, solid chunks of ancient pine tree resin, similar to the insect whose bellyfull of dinosaur blood was supposed to be the source of cloning in the film *Jurassic Park*. Those insects are only 40 millions years old, and since it is thought that dinosaurs died out 65 million years ago, chances are there's no dino blood included!

The 2003 Insect Achievement Awards

There is something about the approach of a new year that causes people and organizations to produce lists. Lists that highlight achievements of the past year. There are lists for every imaginable subject—from fashions to finances, high school sports to world affairs, TV programs to singers. There are good-things lists and not-so-good-things lists. There are so many lists that now we even have lists of the best and worst lists.

So here is my list of the outstanding insect achievements for 2003. May I have the envelope, please?

In the "New Pest Insect of the Year" category, the winner is the emerald ash borer. This metallic green beetle could also be a nominee in the pretti-est insect category. The name suggests that this insect bores in the wood of ash trees, and it does so in the immature stage. As a result, the trees die. The emerald ash borer isn't brand new this year. It was first discovered a few years ago in the Detroit area, where it had arrived from Asia in wood used in pack-ing crates aboard ships. From there, it has been expanding its range as the beetles seek trees on which to lay eggs.

The next category is the "Biggest Nuisance Insect in Homes." The nomi-nees include house fly, boxelder bug, ladybird beetle, and a couple of arthro-pods that are not insects—spiders and millipedes. The winner in this category is the ladybird beetle—not all ladybird beetles, but the multicolored Asian ladybird beetle. It is called multicolored because it ranges in color from tan to red, although it is commonly orange-colored. It also varies in the number of spots, sometimes having none. This beetle arrives at our homes in the late fall, seeking a place to spend the winter. And all winter long, the beetles find their way into our living quarters and make a nuisance of themselves.

The "Most Common Butterfly" category has a clear winner this year. The winner is the painted lady. Painted lady butterflies are also called thistle butterflies or cosmopolitan butterflies. Painted lady refers to their orange-and-black markings; thistle is a reference to the fact that they feed on thistle in the immature stage; and cosmopolitan is because of their worldwide distribution. Painted lady butterflies were everywhere in August and September, sipping nectar from flowers, resting on roadways, and committing suicide on our car grills. As a species, the painted lady occasionally has outbreak years—2003 was one of those years.

The "Most Unexpected Insect Pest" award for 2003 goes to the soybean aphid. The soybean aphid is another new pest in this country that has been causing trouble for soybean growers in Wisconsin and Michigan for the last three years. But this year, the aphid population reached very high numbers in soybean fields in Ohio, Indiana, and Illinois. Because of the high numbers of this insect, we also saw high populations of predatory insects that feed on aphids. That includes the multicolored lady beetle and syrphid flies, which are also called sweat bees by some people.

The biggest insect bust of the year, no doubt, was the severity of the West Nile virus. Even though there were high populations of the mosquito vector of the virus, the incidence of the disease was lower than had been predicted. I'm sure that few people are disappointed that incidence of this disease turned out to be lower than expected.

The final award for 2003 goes to the insect that garnered the most complaints. The winner is the Japanese beetle. Yes, once again, this year the

Japanese beetle is the runaway winner for this award. Not only does the Japanese beetle defoliate a number of our ornamental trees and feed on our fruits and vegetables, but its grubs also destroy our lawns. That also leads to moles in the lawns. So for most homeowners, the Japanese beetle is insect pest no. 1. And if history is any indication, it will probably be the winner again next year—but not by public demand!

A cockroach can live a week without its head. The roach only dies because without a mouth, it can't drink water and dies of thirst.

Bugfolk

We human beings sometimes impart our characteristics to other animals, a process known as anthropomorphism. Through the ages, we have conjured up creatures like the centaur, which was half man and half horse, and the mermaid, a combination of woman and fish. We have even humanized insects, producing creatures that Charles L. Hogue of the Natural History Museum of Los Angeles County calls "Bugfolk."

There aren't, however, many bugfolk, because it's hard for humans to imagine themselves in a form as lowly as an insect. Some of the early bugfolk in human history were merely humans with wings. One of the earliest was the Greek goddess Psyche, who represented the soul. She was depicted as possessing butterfly wings.

Yet Jiminy Cricket is the most recognizable of the bugfolk. Jiminy, that lovable little creature with top hat and umbrella, played a starring role in Disney Studio's film *Pinocchio*. Except for his small size and his ability to sing, Jiminy exhibits few insect characteristics. However, viewers of the film have little doubt that Jiminy is indeed . . . cricket.

Modern cartoonists have made good use of bugfolk. Johnny Hart uses ants frequently in his B.C. comic strip. Hart's ants live in anthills, are sometimes zapped by anteaters, and have insect-like antennae protruding from their heads. When it comes to legs these "antfolk" are more human than insect. Instead of six legs, the insect complement, these creatures have two arms and two legs. That's probably the way it should be, since the ants in

Hart's comic strip are beset with all kinds of human problems, which they address with the full range of human emotions.

Gary Larson is the king of modern cartoonists when it comes to use of bugfolk. Such creatures are commonplace in his Far Side cartoons. Larson's insect characters cover a wide range of types and are anatomically correct with antennae, six legs, two or four wings, mandibles, and distinct body segments. However Larson's insects are folk, because they walk upright and talk. His bugfolk frequently address issues pertinent to insect life, such as shedding of the exoskeleton or food habits, but always with the moral issues that only we mere humans can appreciate.

Bugfolk are showing up in increasing numbers today to help us see ourselves and even get us to consider some profound truths. Of course the real question of a truth learned from a bugfolk is whether the truth was from the insect or the human portion of the creature.

Some States Are Buggy over Insect Symbols

Symbols, it seems, have always been important to states. All states have living symbols. The National Wildlife Federation publishes an official list of such living symbols. It includes birds, mammals, trees, flowers, fish, and insects.

Some states have adopted a plant as an official nickname. For instance, Mississippi is known as The Magnolia State; magnolia just happens to be the state flower. Kansas is known as The Sunflower State, and Nevada, as The Sagebrush State. Both of these plants also are state flowers, although some folks might consider these symbols weeds. Ohio and South Carolina are known for their state trees—the buckeye and the palmetto, respectively.

Some furry mammals also have been adopted as an official state nickname. Oregon is The Beaver State; Minnesota, The Gopher State; and Michigan, The Wolverine State.

All states have official birds, trees, and flowers. However, when it comes to insects, some have an official one and some don't. For instance, Minnesota doesn't have an official state insect. The land of 10,000 lakes does, however, have an unofficial insect—the mosquito, dubbed in curio shops across the state as "The Minnesota State Bird"! I've also noted similar claims relative to the large size of mosquitoes in Florida and Louisiana.

At the present time, about 40 states have official insects. Like birds, trees, and flowers, some states have adopted the same insect as a state symbol. There are 11 states that have the honey bee as their state insect. It is easy to see why state governing bodies would vote for the honey bee as a

state symbol. This insect is hard-working and produces a great product— honey—and in the process provides a desirable ecological service, pollination. Besides, in most honey bee states there is a sizable group of voters known as bee keepers, who no doubt promoted their favorite insect. But as a state symbol, the honey bee has one major drawback. It is not even native to the United States; it was imported from Europe!

Georgia apparently had trouble deciding between insects, so it has an official state insect, the honey bee, and a state butterfly. Butterflies are the state insect in 11 states—12 if you count Georgia. The monarch and swallow-tail each have been adopted by four states. Kentucky has a monarch mimic, the viceroy, as its state insect. The California dog-face butterfly is the choice of another state. (You guessed it, California!) And in Maryland it's the Baltimore checkerspot butterfly that gets to be the state symbol.

Six states have chosen a bright-colored predatory insect—a ladybug— as their state insect. Another famous garden friend, the praying mantis, is the state insect in Connecticut. New Mexico has selected the tarantula hawk wasp as a state symbol. Pennsylvania has adopted a firefly, with the appropriate species name of *pennsylvanicus* for its insect.

Choosing a state insect isn't an easy task. After all, there are so many beautiful and beneficial insects from which to choose. Tennessee solved the problem. They have two state insects, the firefly and the ladybug. They also have a state agricultural insect, the honey bee. Hey, if one state insect is good, three is even better!

Some Pets Not of the Warm and Fuzzy Kind

Humans have kept pets throughout recorded history. Cats or dogs are the companion animals of choice for most people. Some folks have both.

While canines and felines are the most popular pets, other warm-blooded creatures have served the role as well. Rabbits and guinea pigs, for instance. Even rodents are kept as pets. Rats, mice, and hamsters might not appeal to everyone. But then neither does a ferret.

Some people fancy birds as pets. These fine-feathered pets sing, look pretty, and sometimes talk. Fish are popular pets. Fish don't sing or talk and they are not easy to pet. But they are enjoyable to watch. And you don't have to walk your pet fish!

Snakes, lizards, and salamanders are good pets. But many people have trouble thinking of a cold-blooded animal as a pet. Especially those cold-blooded creatures known as arthropods.

Some arthropods, though, are becoming more common as household pets. Insects, spiders, and millipedes are sold and kept as pets.

For many children their very first pet may well have been an insect. A caterpillar discovered wandering on the lawn, or fireflies put in a jar following a merry chase on a warm summer's night. More often than not, such episodes ended in disaster, with a dead insect!

Tarantulas are the most popular of the arthropod pets. There are several reasons for having a spider as a pet. They are unique pets; not everyone has a tarantula. Tarantulas live a long time—15 to 20 years. Some species are easy to handle. And, well, tarantulas are interesting creatures.

Scorpions, like spiders, are also arachnids, and some are also kept as pets. The sting of a scorpion and the bite of a tarantula are poisonous, so these pets must be handled with care. Indeed, petting an arachnid is not something most owners do.

Some pet stores sell giant tropical millipedes. These multi-legged worm-like creatures are just large relatives of the millipedes we find in our compost pile. Like the local millipedes, these creatures feed on dead plant material. They are part of nature's recycling crew. While millipedes are safe, unusual pets, the same is not true of the centipedes. Centipedes are predators and have a poisonous bite.

Cockroaches are not an insect that people like to have in their homes. The Madagascar hissing cockroach is an occasional exception. This cockroach gets its name because it is found in Madagascar and makes a hissing sound when disturbed. That sound, combined with two eye-like protuberances on the front part of its body, allows the insect to mimic a snake.

The Madagascar hissing roach is a recycler in nature. So people who have them as pets feed them almost anything. Dry dog food works well. But don't forget the water. Cockroaches, like other animals, need water.

Madagascar roaches are the largest cockroaches in the world by weight. So having one for a pet allows the owner to brag about having the largest roaches in the world in his house! Not something many people would like to brag about, I'm sure.

The nice thing about a roach is that you don't have to have someone care for your pet when you go on vacation. Give it extra food and water and it will be fine when you return. But be sure to keep the lid on the container, otherwise your pet might have decided to live in the sofa or kitchen cabinet!

Honey Hunters Have Raided Nests for Eons

Humans have recognized for eons that honey is as good a food for them as it is for the bees that made it.

There are several references to honey consumption in the Bible. For instance, John the Baptist, while he was wandering in the wilderness, consumed wild honey. Samson once robbed a bee colony of enough honey for a snack when he and his parents were traveling along the road to Timnath.

No one really knows how long ago humans began consuming honey, but it was no doubt long before John the Baptist and Samson walked the earth. A painting, estimated to be about 7,000 years old, on the walls of a rock shelter in eastern Spain near Valencia clearly depicts a person gathering honey.

The earliest collection of honey probably involved robbing the nests bees had constructed in hollow trees or rock crevices. A necessary preliminary to such thievery was the discovery of the nest. It is reasonable to assume that ancient humans actively searched for the nests of bees in much the same way they might have hunted animals or looked for fruiting plants.

Bee hunting is still practiced in some parts of the world, and was common in the United States as recently as the 1940s. Observing the flight direction of bees moving in and out of patches of flowers is helpful in locating the general vicinity of the nest. Finding the exact location is sometimes more difficult. As an aid to locating the nest site, bee hunters have sometimes

resorted to using a white powder such as flour to dust bees caught visiting flowers. The idea is that the marked bees then will leave some of the powder on the entrance of the nest, such as a hole in a tree, making it easier to see.

Humans aren't the only animals that have a sweet tooth. A number of creatures are known to eat honey when the opportunity arises. Bears are widely recognized as honey eaters and will actively seek bee nests in order to rob them.

One of the most interesting of the honey-eating animals is a bird. There is a small, plainly colored African bird named the honey guide. This bird got its name because it leads humans or other animals to bee nests. The honey guide bird gets its reward by sharing in the honey exposed when the creature it led to the spot tears into the bee nest.

Bees don't store honey for the benefit of the rest of the animal kingdom, and they don't share willingly the fruits of their labor. We humans and other animals that would have a little taste of honey no doubt discovered very quickly, as this ancient proverb states: "He who would gather honey must bear the sting of the bees."

Insect Names Have Interesting Histories

Humans have always had a passion for naming things. Names are essential to language. They allow us to communicate about things and each other.

Some names, like "rocks," "plants," and "insects," describe large groups of similar things. These are divided into smaller, more specific groups with other names. Thus, some plants are trees and some insects are butterflies.

But all trees and all butterflies are not the same. So these groups are further divided and given other names. The names used in everyday language are known as common names. Each animal and plant species also has a two-word scientific name that is often based on Latin.

Scientific and common names of living things frequently reflect characteristics of the organism, such as behavior or looks. Or a name might reveal some now-forgotten bit of history that led to the name; such is the case with insect common names.

The basis for some insect names is obvious. Grasshoppers consume grass and use their back legs to hop. Frog hoppers are a type of insect known as tree hoppers. If you guessed that tree hoppers commonly can be found in trees exhibiting a hopping motion, you are correct.

Many insects have "fly" in their names, recognizing the power of flight of these creatures. An entire group of insects is called "flies." One is common in houses, the house fly. Other fly names indicate a favorite host, such as the horse fly and deer fly. Some fly names even suggest a target site on the animal. The face fly and heel fly that attack cattle come to mind.

Many insects have "fly" in their names but scientifically are not really flies, although they do fly. Confused? Consider the butterfly. Butterflies certainly wing about and the name suggests an association with springtime, a time also known as the butter season. Lanternflies presumably were attracted to the light of an old-time lantern. Mayflies emerge in great numbers during that month of the year. Harvestflies, also known as cicadas, are common during the fall harvest season. One type of cicada is known as the dogday cicada because of high populations during the "dog days" of summer.

One of the most widely recognized and generally admired insects is known as the ladybug. There are many types of ladybugs that vary in color and number of spots. And they are not all female! Half of the ladybugs are males. The name is based on a control approach for aphids feeding on the flax crop in England during the Middle Ages. History records that people of those days would pray to the Virgin Mary for help with the pesky little aphids. Their prayers would be answered when aphid-eating insects showed up. The beneficial insect was dubbed "our lady's bug." Today, these insects are still known as ladybugs or ladybird beetles.

Other common names reflect some unusual behavior of the insects. One such insect is known as the doodlebug. The doodlebug is also known as an ant lion. The doodlebug name is based on its erratic side-to-side crawling behavior. Ant lion comes from its aggressive feeding behavior as it consumes ants that fall into the soil pit where it lives.

The giant water bug in modern times has been called the electric light bug. This insect leaves lakes, streams, and ponds during the night to seek new habitats. The bright lights of the city beckon, and the insect ends up around a mercury vapor light illuminating a parking lot.

A well-known insect of times past is the dung beetle. Dung beetles in

general are recyclers of mammal manure, which they fashion in balls and bury as food for their offspring. One feeds on cow manure. These black beetles are known for pushing and pulling dust-covered balls of cow manure along cow paths in the pasture. The process frequently result in the beetles losing their grip on the ball, which causes them to tumble down. Hence, these insects are known in some localities as tumblebugs. Not exactly the most glorious name, but, then, neither is their role in nature!

The world's largest roach (which lives in South America) is six inches long with a one-foot wingspan.

Flea Glass Apt Name for a Microscope

An unknown entomologist once stated that insects are big enough to see, but not big enough to see well. That comment speaks volumes about human-insect interaction.

The microscope showed us insects in a new light. Galileo is known for his work with the telescope, but when he looked through the other end of the device he had a microscope. While he was not a biologist, the earliest biological observation with a microscope is credited to Galileo. He is said to have reported that each eye of a small animal is "perforated with holes to afford passage to the images of visible things." Galileo was describing the compound eye of an insect.

In the early days of its use, the microscope was called a flea glass. In 1693, Antony van Leeuwenhoek described the metamorphosis of the flea. He drew detailed pictures of egg, larvae, pupa, and adult. He even described a minute mite parasite on the larva. This observation probably gave rise to the Jonathan Swift lines:

> So naturalists observe, a flea
> Has smaller fleas that on him prey;
> And these have smaller still to bite 'em;
> And so proceed ad infinitum.

The microscope has allowed scientists to clearly look at very small insects. But some people prefer not to see the teeth on a flea. They would just as soon not know that much about something that will take a bite when it gets the chance.

Lepidoptera

Professor
Buggy
circa 1904

Butterflies and moths are classified in the insect order Lepidoptera. This order name literally means "scale wing." Lepidoptera is a very descriptive name for this group of insects, because their wings are almost always covered with scales. This fact has been discovered by almost anyone who has ever picked up an adult butterfly or moth and ended up with scales on their fingers. The mouth of adult moths and butterflies is a tube affair called a proboscis. When not in use, the proboscis of a butterfly or moth is coiled up and hidden. This tube allows the insect to imbibe liquids such as nectar or water or in some instances fluids oozing from rotting animal carcasses.

Around 160,000 species of Lepidoptera have been identified worldwide. North America is home to around 16,000 species of butterflies and moths. Based on number of species, there are far more moths than butterflies. For instance, there have been 149 species of butterflies identified in Indiana, while probably over 1,200 species of moths are found in the state.

Butterflies are no doubt the most recognized and most appreciated group of nature's six-legged creatures. All butterflies are active during daylight hours and have been described as nature's flying flowers. It is an apt comparison, because the bright colors and marking patterns of butterflies rival that of some of the brightest colored and most ornate flowers. Some people are so enamored with butterflies that they cultivate butterfly gardens to attract them, maintain butterfly feeders to feed them, or pay admission to commercial butterfly houses to observe them. Butterflies are also commonly used for decorative purposes, including a very popular human tattoo item.

Moths are the other major group of Lepidoptera and they are mostly

active during the night hours. Unlike butterflies, most species of moths are dull-colored, like most other night-active animals. Biologically the dull color patterns allow moths to blend into the environment during the day. It helps them avoid becoming a meal for day-active insect predators. However, a few species of moths are day-flyers and generally exhibit bright coloration that many times makes them resemble bees.

Butterflies and moths are both called caterpillars in their immature stages. Caterpillars are wormlike creatures with chewing mouthparts. Most caterpillars feed on plants, and because of that some species are major crop pests. Caterpillars appear to have more than the six legs that are characteristic of insects. The other leg-like structures function much like legs but are called prolegs. Prolegs help caterpillars keep a good grip on their food plants.

Many caterpillars are green and blend in so well with plants that they often go unnoticed. Others have bright colors, including stripes and spots. Such coloration, like that of the monarch butterfly larva, generally sends a warning message "If you eat me, I'll leave a bad taste in your mouth!" Some caterpillars are fuzzy; others are smooth-skinned. As a general rule, fuzzy caterpillars turn into moths, while the hairless ones become butterflies.

Lepidoptera, like many other insects have four stages during their life: egg, larva, pupa, and adult. Moth pupae are generally covered with silk. It is from the covering of the pupa of the silkworm that the unwound silk fiber is used to produce silk thread. Butterfly pupae, on the other hand, are not covered in silk. Scientists call such pupae naked.

One of the largest insects by measure in the world is a butterfly. Queen Alexandra's birdwing butterfly measures 30 centimeters (12 inches) from wingtip to wingtip and is found in New Guinea. Some of the smallest of all insects are moths, and a few species measure less than 6 millimeters (¼ inch). Scientists for good reason call these insects microlepidoptera. We notice the large showy Lepidoptera. We don't pay much attention to the smaller or dull-colored insects of that order—unless of course these insects just happen to be caterpillars feeding on our garden or crop plants or chewing holes in our woolen clothing.

Butterflies' wings may be small and delicate, but some people believe they can have a big effect on the world. The so-called "butterfly effect" claims that small events can ripple out and have big impact, so that if a butterfly flapped its wings in Asia, it could change the course of a tornado in Kansas. Science doesn't support this theory, but that doesn't keep it out of pop culture—it was the subject of the 2004 film starring Ashton Kutcher, *The Butterfly Effect.*

Butterflies Are Favorite Insects for Most People

Most people don't care much for insects. An exception is the insect that some poets have called a flying flower. Yes, almost everyone has a soft spot in his or her heart for butterflies.

If any insect group is perceived by humans to be warm and fuzzy, it is the butterflies. Butterflies really aren't warm, though. Like all insects, they are cold-blooded. But they are fuzzy! Butterflies, and their insect cousins the moths, have fuzzy wings.

Butterflies and moths are classified in the same insect order. The order name, Lepidoptera, reflects the fuzzy nature of their wings. It means "scale wing."

There are roughly 10 times as many species of moths as butterflies, but most people are more familiar with the butterflies. That is partially because butterflies are active during the day while moths are active at night. In addition, butterflies are mostly bright-colored. Moths tend to be somewhat drab. Consequently, people are more likely to notice butterflies than moths.

The color of butterfly wings is achieved in one of two ways. Some of the color is in pigments, much as it is in most other animals. In addition, color in some of the brighter butterflies—and a few other insects—is due to light reflection. In butterflies, small parallel ridges on the wing scales break up the light into component parts. Water droplets in the air do the same thing to light when a rainbow is produced.

The color of the beautiful morpho butterflies of the Amazon is produced in this way. Because the color is the result of light reflection, the color changes when these butterflies move their wings. Many morphos are a bright, metallic blue when the wings are held out from the body. When held vertically, however, the bright color disappears and the wings appear a brownish gray.

Morpho butterflies tend to slowly open and close their wings when at rest. Because the color changes as the wings move, the behavior works to confuse a potential predator, which might be considering a butterfly meal. The butterfly is playing a now-you-see-me, now-you-don't game with the predator.

The same effect is achieved by butterflies that have bright colors on the outside of their wings but duller colors on the underside. When the wings are folded, such as when the butterfly is resting, the color pattern may allow the insect to blend into the environment. Such is the case with the angle-wing butterflies. These butterflies are medium-sized and have a reddish-brown color with black spots. The undersurface of their wings is gray and brown, colors that imitate bark and dry leaves.

Butterflies are often named after the way their wings look. Most people would recognize that swallowtail butterflies are named after the projection which looks like the tail of a bird known as a swallow, found on the hind wings.

The angle-wings have wing margins that are scalloped and indented as if they had been cut with scissors.

The whites and sulfurs are common butterflies, with names based on the color of their wings. There is a group of butterflies called the purples, and—you guessed it—they are purple in color. There is a banded purple, a spotted purple, and a great purple hairstreak.

Peacock butterflies are dusky brown in color but have eyespots on the wings, similar to those found in the feathers of peacocks. Another group of brown-colored butterflies is the tortoise shells. Of course, their wing pattern reminds folks of the shell of a tortoise.

What is it that people like about butterflies? It might be the bright colors. Maybe it is their delicate nature. It might be the fact that they visit our gardens. But I suspect that people really like butterflies because—unlike some other insects—these flying flowers can't bite or sting!

> It is a misdemeanor to kill or threaten a butterfly—so says City Ordinance No. 352 in Pacific Grove, California.

Butterfly or Moth?

Scientifically, butterflies and moths are close relatives. They are classified as Lepidoptera. If the order name Lepidoptera sounds a bit like Greek to you, that's because it is. Like many scientific names, Lepidoptera is based on Greek terms. The first part, *lepidos,* means "scale." It is the basis for the word "leprosy," a human disease that results in scaling skin. Combine *lepidos* with the Greek word for wing, *ptera,* and we get the word Lepidoptera.

Literally, then, butterflies and moths are the scale-wing insects. It is an appropriate scientific name for these insects, since one of their most recognizable characteristics is their scaled wings. Almost anyone who has ever caught, or attempted to catch, a butterfly or moth has found that the wing scales rub off rather easily.

In addition to the basis for their name, butterflies and moths also share other characteristics. For instance, adults of both have coiled tubes for mouths. These tubes are used for imbibing liquids, most often the nectar from flowers or water. As immatures, the Lepidoptera are known as caterpillars, and all have chewing mouths that are used to chow down on their favorite food, which is most often the foliage of plants.

There are, however, major differences between butterflies and moths. First, they fly at different times. Butterflies are out and about during the daylight hours. Moths, on the other hand, fly at night. These activity patterns relate to the fact that butterflies tend to be brightly colored, while moths are dull colored. After all, it doesn't seem appropriate to dress in showy clothing if you are not going to be seen, as is the case for most moths.

Moths also have fuzzy antennae. Butterflies have hairless antennae, many times with a knob at the end. Moths tend to rest with their wings held horizontally over their backs. Butterflies rest with their wings held vertically. In flight, butterflies tend to glide or float. Moths seem to be in a hurry and keep flapping their wings.

As for body shape, moths and butterflies could serve as the before-and-after examples for a weight-loss advertisement. The moth, with its rather stout build, would serve as the "before"; the slender butterfly could be the "after."

But those aren't the only differences. Even the caterpillars look different. Generally the caterpillars of moths are hairy, and the caterpillars of butterflies are clean-shaven. The same is true of these insects when the larvae turn into pupae. Moth pupae tend to be covered, many times with silk. The silkworm is a prime example. The butterfly, on the other hand, has a naked pupa.

Of course, there are exceptions to all of these rules. A few moths fly during the daytime and even have bright-colored wings. And to make matters worse, some butterflies fly more like moths than butterflies. Nonetheless, they are all still Lepidoptera!

Butterflies at Weddings, Oh My!

June has always been considered the month for weddings. There was just something special about being a June bride, I guess. One wag says that the month of June was a favorite month for weddings because that's when people historically started taking regular baths again after a long hard winter. And one is to presume that clean brides and grooms were off to a good start in their married life.

Recently, however, the other end of summer, August, has dethroned June as our favorite month to get hitched. Yes, a little more than 10 percent of U.S. weddings are held in the heat of August. June is second, with 9.9 percent of the annual weddings.

Statistics aside, I still think of June as the wedding month. At least, that is, when I receive inquiries about releasing butterflies as part of the ceremony. Of course, such a question would probably not even be considered for a December wedding. When asked about using butterflies at a wedding, I always respond with a question of my own: "What is wrong with rose petals or rice?"

There is just something about the beauty of fluttering butterflies that captures the imagination of brides-to-be. I am never asked by grooms-to-be about using butterflies at weddings. That may be because grooms are just not interested in butterflies or have very little say in weddings. Or both.

I'm not sure where this thing about releasing butterflies at weddings got started. There was a movie called *Angels & Insects* that included a

wedding scene with butterflies fluttering around. It was appropriate for that movie wedding, set in Victorian times. Especially since the groom was a naturalist specializing in those beautiful blue morpho butterflies from the Amazon.

I discourage the use of butterflies at weddings. It's not because I like the traditional tossing of rice that much. And, goodness knows, I would enjoy the sight of fluttering butterflies as much as anyone at a wedding. But the problems outweigh the benefits.

Problem No. 1 is where can you get butterflies for release at weddings. Such an activity is popular enough that several suppliers are listed on the Internet. At $10 per scale-winged flapper, the cost can add up quickly. Especially since a dozen—and they might be somewhat cheaper by the dozen—butterflies do not provide much of an aerial display. So you will need several hundred to make the release worthwhile. Now we are talking quite a few dollars, just for the insects.

If you don't purchase your butterflies, it might be possible to collect your own. I can't imagine many brides and their mothers wanting to grab butterfly nets and run over meadow and byway on the day before the big event.

Or you could raise your own butterflies. But that has the problem of getting the adults to emerge at just the right time—the day before the wedding. If you fail in the timing, you might get the wedding guests to enjoy watching a few caterpillars crawl down the aisle.

An additional problem is keeping the butterflies alive up to the time of the release. It is not a very pleasant sight when the butterflies are tossed up in the air and half fall lifeless to the ground. And besides, live butterflies don't always fly on command, especially when they have been confined.

Additionally, many butterfly biologists have been opposed to such releases because there is the possibility of releasing non-native species into an area. That is how new pests sometimes get started. And even butterflies that are native to the area could introduce new genetics or diseases that might cause the natural populations to be harmed.

Maybe that is why more weddings are being held outdoors in August. This is the time when natural butterfly populations are at their peak, and nature might just provide the real thing. Along with mosquitoes, of course! Hey, you can't expect everything to be perfect for a wedding.

Charles Valentine Riley, one of the early U.S. federal entomologists, is widely credited with efforts to introduce a ladybird beetle predator to control the cottony cushion scale pest of citrus in California. The predatory insect was the Vedalia beetle, and C. V. Riley named his daughter Catherine Vedalia Riley after the insect.

Beautiful but Bitter

It's yellow, black, and white-striped in youth, has 14 leg-like appendages, fearsome mandibles, and a hard-shell head. It feeds on a plant that contains chemicals used as medicine. Later, as an adult, it's brown with black stripes, and spends the winter in a remote mountainous region of Mexico. Could it be an invader from outer space or a creature from the black lagoon?

Well, actually, it's the monarch butterfly! One of our best-known insects. The bright, striped colors of the larva warns potential predators that it's distasteful.

The bitter taste of the larva comes from the juice of the milkweed plant that it uses for food. The milkweed plant contains bitter substances called cardiac glycosides, which are named for their use as a human heart medicine. These compounds benefit the milkweed plant by acting as antifeeding compounds for most animals, including insects.

The monarch, however, has developed the ability to utilize the plant in spite of the presence of the bitter chemicals. The larva stores the toxic compounds in its body. This makes the larva bad-tasting, an attribute that is transferred to the adult following pupation.

Many birds are predators of insects, but they can't tolerate the bitter taste of the monarch. To advertise their bad taste, the monarch, in both the adult and larval stages, wears bright colors. So effective is the scheme that the viceroy butterfly, a good-tasting insect that resembles the monarch in color and pattern, also is protected.

The monarch, actually a tropical butterfly, has adapted to more northern climates by leaving the winter behind. Each fall monarchs leisurely flutter toward overwintering areas in the mountains of Mexico.

Along the way, great flocks of these insects sometimes gather on trees to rest overnight. These resting sites, called butterfly trees, are one of nature's truly memorable sights.

The monarch butterfly is indeed a biological miracle. These fragile insects wing over 1,000 miles to a place they've never been. Come spring they head north to lay eggs on plants too toxic for most animals to eat.

Once egg laying is complete, the butterflies die, leaving the younger generation to carry on. Each succeeding generation moves northward to lay eggs until their genetic code unerringly indicates that it's time to turn around.

The butterflies begin the long and treacherous southern journey. They make the trip not so much for themselves, but to ensure the survival of the future generations of the "beautiful but bitter" monarch.

Butterfly Garden: Build It and They Will Come

Adult butterflies are insects that most people appreciate. So much so, in fact, that some people plant gardens, known as butterfly gardens, designed to attract these beautiful insects.

A successful butterfly garden is one that contains all the things that butterflies need to be successful. As for most animals, an important aspect of life for butterflies is food. Nectar is a primary food for most butterflies. Many kinds of plants have flowers that provide nectar for butterflies. These are the plants we like to have in our gardens because they have brightly colored blossoms. Flowers really don't exist to please humans, however; they are there to attract insects.

Nectar flowers exist in many shapes. Flowers known as composites, such as daisies and marigolds, have a shape such that butterflies can actually perch on the blossom as they sip the nectar. Other good nectar flowers have closely packed clusters of flowers. One such flower is buddleia, also known appropriately as the butterfly bush. Honeysuckle is a vine, and its name suggests it might be attractive to butterflies. It is. Such things as daylilies, with large single flowers, are also good nectar sources.

Every beautiful butterfly is preceded by a caterpillar stage. Butterfly caterpillars are plant foliage eaters and, because of this habit, sometimes cause damage to plants. However, successful butterfly gardeners have some plants for butterfly caterpillar food. For instance, milkweeds are the food for the monarch butterfly caterpillar.

Some butterfly names suggest the kind of food their caterpillars eat. The pipe vine swallowtail feeds on pipe vine and the spicebush swallowtail on, you guessed it, spicebush. Queen-Anne's lace and parsley will attract the black swallowtail. Those white cabbage butterflies begin their lives as caterpillars feeding on cabbage or a related plant.

While some of these caterpillars can interfere with the success of plants we were planning to eat, the successful butterfly gardener finds some way to allow the caterpillars to have their share. One thing to remember is to eliminate insecticide use from the butterfly garden, otherwise you are likely to end up killing the caterpillar that will become the beautiful butterfly.

Other considerations for a successful butterfly garden other than food include water and abundant sunlight. Insects are cold-blooded and need sunlight to provide the warmth they need to function. Butterflies also require places to rest and spend the night. Shrub foliage is useful for this purpose, as are overgrown areas and patches of tall grass. Some people actually build a butterfly log pile to provide a shelter.

A line from the movie *Field of Dreams* is appropriate to butterfly gardens. Build it and they will come! You'll be glad you did.

A Tale of Two Moths

The end-of-year holidays are marked by many traditional activities. Thanksgiving feasting, trimming the tree, and lighting holiday candles all add excitement to the season.

All of this is sometimes accompanied by another, some would say less festive, holiday scene. It's the time-honored activity that could be known as the "chasing of the moths." A classic story, it is reenacted time and time again in many households across America. It begins with an unconfirmed sighting—a little brown moth fluttering about in the glare of the kitchen or living room lights. The erratic flight ends up with a landing on cabinet or curtain.

To most homeowners, the presence of little brown moths is disquieting—something outside the benevolent spirit of the season. It spells trouble with a capital T. Little brown moths, you see, are known, in their immature or larval stages, to feed on clothes or in stored food. Either way, a moth could mean trouble.

Moth sightings are frequently followed by a commotion of high intensity as homeowners try to kill the offending insect. Killing the moth is really only the first volley of an all-out war. What normally follows is a seek-and-destroy mission that would please any retired military officer.

Unless the moth was found near clothing, it is a good bet that the little beast began life in some stored food item. Let the search begin! Such things as oatmeal or cornmeal are immediately suspect and should be dragged from the deep, dark recesses of the food cupboard for a quick look-see. One should not forget that most spices are also potential food items for these insects, as are dry dog and cat foods.

The most common of the little brown moths that frequently cause consternation for cooks are the Angoumois grain moth and the Indian-meal moth. The Angoumois grain moth has a rather highfalutin'-sounding French name. However, as it feeds it frequently leaves behind unsightly silken webs not at all in tune with the obvious continental sophistication suggested by its name!

The Indian-meal moth gets its name because it was first identified feeding in the grain meal produced by the early European settlers to the United States. The meal had been produced from Indian corn, the maize crop named after the misidentified Native American peoples growing it when Europeans arrived on this continent. Hence the insect became the Indian-meal moth and, to this day, makes its meal out of our meals-to-be—grain meal, that is.

Both of these insects can feed in the dried flower arrangements that frequently adorn our homes in this holiday season. So if little brown moths are seen fluttering to and fro in your home during the holidays, don't throw out all the food in the cupboard. At least not until you have concluded that the unwanted moths are not emerging from the dried-plant holiday wreath. Happy Holidays!

Caterpillar Encounters Escalate during Fall Months

Most people enjoy encounters with butterflies. These living flowers add dabs of color and whimsy to our gardens and roadsides. But we aren't as fond of moths and caterpillars. Moths are drab and reclusive, and caterpillars have been described as nothing more than creeping plant chompers.

When the calendar rolls around to August and September, caterpillars are likely to creep from their summer hiding places and into our lives. Yes, the fall season brings with it numerous encounters of the caterpillar kind.

Immature butterflies and moths are both called caterpillars. The word "caterpillar" is based on the Latin *catta pilosa,* which means "hairy cat." It seems likely that the term "caterpillar" was first used for immatures of moths. That is because moth caterpillars are often hairy—covered with hair and spines.

Scientists note that the amount of hair that a caterpillar possesses might be a hint as to whether it is to become a butterfly or moth. Butterfly caterpillars are hairless, while moth caterpillars tend to be hairy. But several species of moths have caterpillars that are smooth-skinned and without hair. So when you discover a hairy caterpillar, you can be certain that it will turn out to be a moth. A smooth caterpillar will probably become a butterfly, but not always!

Some of the most recognizable moths spend their immature days crawling around as hairless caterpillars. These include the flower-feeding moths known as hummingbird moths. Their caterpillars are called hornworms and are very smooth-skinned, as anyone who has picked one off a tomato plant knows.

It is the hairy caterpillars that really attract our attention. Some of the most noticeable are immatures of what are called the giant silkworm moths. These are the cecropia, promethea, and polyphemus moths. Their larvae are not fuzzy, but they are large caterpillars. Each is nearly 3 inches in length. Their size, combined with an assortment of spines and knobs, results in rather impressive-looking caterpillars.

There are three species of the giant silkworm moths common in the eastern United States. These caterpillars feed on the leaves of hardwood trees. One is the cecropia. Its larvae are green-colored with studded protrusions on each segment. The polyphemus caterpillar is also green-colored but lacks the studded protrusions. It does have tufts of spines emerging from red spots. The promethea caterpillar is bluish-green in color and has two short, red horns near the head.

A striking large, green moth with long tails, the luna moth, has a caterpillar that resembles those of the giant silkworm moths. It also is green in color with red-marked tuffs of bristles on each segment.

Probably the most fearsome looking of the giant caterpillars is that of the regal moth. This caterpillar has large, red, curved horns near the head. It is appropriately called the hickory-horned devil!

The caterpillars of the giant moths are harmless. They look fearsome and sometimes act as if they are trying to bite. There are hairy caterpillars that really are dangerous because they have stinging spines or hairs. One such is the Io moth. This green caterpillar has a red-and-white stripe along the side.

Another stinging caterpillar is called the saddleback. These caterpillars are slug-shaped and green in color with a brown-and-white saddle-shaped

mark across the middle. The easily recognized color pattern is called warning coloration, because the caterpillar spines will produce skin irritation when handled.

Other fuzzy caterpillars that are noticeable in the fall have been touted as winter-weather predictors. These so-called woollybears are said to predict the severity of the winter, based on thickness of the coat, width of the black band, or direction of travel. The only thing that the woollybear caterpillar can predict with accuracy is that winter is on the way.

When fall arrives, all caterpillars stop feeding and crawl around looking for a place to hibernate. The process is called wandering. So when you encounter a wandering caterpillar, the best advice is look but don't touch. After all, some of those fuzzy caterpillars are armed with stinging hairs.

A Very Good Year for Painted Lady Butterflies

To borrow a line from a song made famous by Frank Sinatra, "It was a very good year!" Such a line could apply to wine, to winning sports teams, or even to the stock market. This year, it certainly applies to painted lady butterflies, at least in the Midwest.

Painted lady butterflies seem to be everywhere. They are so common on flowers that, when disturbed, the uprising resembles a dust storm. Roads are covered with resting painted ladies. So much so that a drive in the country often results in a car grill clogged with painted lady carcasses.

The painted lady is about two inches from wing tip to wing tip. It is orange-colored with black patches and black wing tips. It also has four eye spots on the back side of the hind wing. Painted ladies are one of the most common butterfly species in the world. That is why they also are known as the cosmopolitan butterfly. Painted ladies are found in temperate regions around the world, except South America and Australia.

Even though the painted lady is widespread in temperate regions, it cannot survive cold winters. These butterflies die off each winter in North America, except in the Southwest. Each spring, these orange-and-black butterflies migrate northward. Before the growing season is over, they can be found everywhere, except the most northern areas of Canada and Alaska.

How do the butterfly populations build up so quickly? First, they have a variety of food plants. The painted lady caterpillars can be found feeding on many species of wildflowers. They are especially common on thistle. In fact,

painted ladies were once known as thistle butterflies. Their populations can also build up rapidly because they can go through several generations per year.

Because the populations can reach very high numbers in a short period of time, the caterpillars have been known to defoliate their food plants. One food plant is the soybean. When painted lady caterpillars are filling their guts on this crop plant, they would be considered pests. But to the delight of farmers, such an occasion is rare. Farmers would much rather see these insects feeding on thistles!

Painted lady butterflies also are reared in the classroom to demonstrate the metamorphosis of insects. In the classroom, the caterpillars feed on an artificial diet that resembles solid pea soup with some fiber in it. Once the caterpillar has completed feeding, it attaches itself to the lid of the container to form the pupa. In the wild, the pupa would be attached to the underside of a leaf or stem. Following emergence from the pupa, the butterflies mate and lay eggs. The complete life cycle takes less than three weeks.

The painted lady was given a scientific name by Linnaeus, the founder of the system of binomial nomenclature—the practice of giving a genus and species name to all living things. The name selected was *Vanessa cardui.* "Vanessa" is the Old English word for "butterfly," probably based on the ancient goddess Venus. "Cardui" is based on "cardu," which is Latin for "thistle," so the name means "butterfly of thistle"!

Insect Armies on the March

They don't have drill sergeants, barracks or boot camps. But they behave very much like armies. That's why they are called armyworms.

These caterpillars have gained their common name primarily because of their habit of marching, like an army, in great numbers from location to location.

In addition, these worms appear to use a military tactic of surprise strikes. Armyworms can also use an army-like tactic of destroying everything in their path.

When armyworm populations are high, they move from place to place. Sometimes roadways are literally covered with crawling caterpillars. Large-scale movement is generally associated with the search for new plants on which to feed. Large populations can quickly devour the available leafy-green material in an area. The hungry caterpillars then march off in search of food.

Armyworm damage doesn't just appear overnight. Like all insects, the caterpillars begin life as an egg. In fact, each caterpillar can have as many as 500 brothers and sisters. That is one reason why populations and damage can show up very quickly.

Adult armyworms are brown-colored moths. These moths constitute the air corps of this insect army. The moths wing their way, sometimes riding weather fronts, into Midwestern states early each spring.

The female moth then fastens her eggs onto leaves of grass plants. The

eggs hatch in a couple of weeks, and the young caterpillars begin feeding. But like little kids, they have a little appetite—at least compared to the teen-age caterpillars that follow. In the last two weeks of their caterpillar life, the true meaning of "the hungry caterpillar" surfaces. They can at this time "eat themselves out of house and home"!

The damage to plants during this feeding frenzy can be substantial. Grassy pastures can be eaten down. Young corn plants can be chewed to a stub, and wheat can be totally defoliated. Sometimes the hungry caterpillars can clip the heads of wheat so that they end up on the ground.

In general, it is grassy plants like wheat, oats, fescue, and corn that are damaged. Armyworms only feed on non-grass plants, like soybeans, when they have eaten all the available grasses.

Once it has completed feeding, the caterpillar crawls into the ground and pupates. In about two weeks, a new armyworm moth appears, and the cycle of the armyworm continues. There are two or three generations in northern states, but it is the first one that causes most of the damage.

There are actually several insects that are called armyworms. They are all moths and behave in a similar way as caterpillars. One is called the true armyworm. These are the ones that cause damage to plants in May and June.

There is an insect known as the army cutworm, which also sometimes begins the marching habit. Fall armyworms, as the name suggests, develop later in the season than do true armyworms. They have been known to consume all the leaf surface of mature corn plants, leaving only the mid-veins of the leaves. To add insult to injury, they sometimes attack the ears of corn as well.

Armyworms can disappear as quickly as they appear, because they can be attacked by other insects or diseases. These opposing armies wage a battle

against the invading forces of the armyworms. Mother Nature has a way of making sure things don't get too far out of hand—even with something as fearsome as an army of worms!

Monarch caterpillars shed their skin four times before they become a chrysalis, growing over 2700 times their original size.

Moths' Bright Underwings Startle Predators

Catocala moths are among the largest and showiest of North American moths. These moths are widely known by the common name "underwings." The name "underwing" is very descriptive. In general, underwing moths appear much as any other moth, with nondescript brown or gray mottled forewings.

Unlike most moths, the hindwings, or underwings, of catocala are brightly colored. The scientific name *Catocala* literally means "beautiful below." Frequently the hindwings are striped with black bands alternating with orange or red bands. Since the underwing moths, like most other moths, are night-flying insects, the bright colors are not often seen, except when the insect is displayed in a collection.

While not often visible, the colored wings of the underwing moths have an important biological function. Underwing moths are subject to predation by birds. As a first line of defense, the moth uses the cryptic coloration of the forewings to blend into the environment, specifically the bark of a tree on which it rests during the daylight hours.

It is generally assumed that the brightly colored underwings serve to frighten predators if the insect is discovered. The sudden display of bright colors results in a startled response by birds and might provide an opportunity for the moth to escape becoming a meal. It is also possible that the colors serve a deflective function, causing the bird to direct its pecking to the hind-wings rather than the biologically more important body of the insect.

The striking contrast between the forewings and the hindwings of these moths fascinates most viewers. But Theodore Sargent, in his book *Legion of Night the Underwing Moths,* states that the common names of the moths are at least as intriguing as their beauty. Moths are frequently associated with night, mystery, and death, so we have the dejected underwing and the inconsolable underwing. We also have the mourning underwing and the foresaken underwing.

Also in the sad vein is the widow underwing. Other names relate to love and marriage, such as the betrothed underwing, the consort underwing, and the mother underwing. We also have the sweetheart underwing and the bride underwing, which should not be confused with the old maid underwing.

Nearly all of the older *Catocala* names are female names from the Bible, Shakespeare, Russian folklore and Greek mythology. From Roman history we find virtuous women such as Irene and the not-so-virtuous, such as Delilah and Cleopatra.

Why so many references to female names in this group of insects? It just might be that the men who described each beautiful and mysterious moth were reminded of some of their female acquaintances of the human species.

Tenting on the Old Campground

For many folks, spring means the return of the camping season. It's time to retrieve the musty-smelling tent from the basement or attic. But before most human campers make their first spring foray into the great out-of-doors, the insect tents are already in place.

The most conspicuous of the insect tentmakers is the eastern tent caterpillar. This insect, a hairy brown caterpillar that grows to about 2 inches in length, has been observed making tents in America's trees since 1646.

The insect passes the winter in the egg stage. In early spring, the eggs hatch. Young larvae band together and produce a large thick web, called a tent. The tent is normally located in the fork of a tree.

Larvae do not feed within the tent. They use the tent for protection from the weather and possibly from predators. Hungry larvae leave the tent and feed on the newly forming leaves of their host trees. Favorite trees are wild cherry, apple, peach, and plum, although other trees are sometimes attacked.

By midsummer, the larvae pupate and turn into yellowish brown moths. The moths mate and lay clusters of eggs, which will hatch the next spring to start the cycle over again.

Some people, it seems, do not like the sight of a group of happy campers—at least of the insect variety—so they try to dispose of the little beasts. If the tree under attack is small, one approach is to prune the limb with the web and worms and destroy it. Several insecticides can also be used to kill the caterpillars. However, treating large trees with insecticide requires specialized equipment, so it may be necessary to hire a professional.

In general, the feeding of tent caterpillars will not cause permanent harm to a tree. Usually the tree will have time to leaf out following the feeding. However, defoliation by tent caterpillars in two or more consecutive years could stress the plant and warrant control.

So the damage caused is more to the aesthetics of the tree and the pride of the owner. However, some people take the approach that a few insect tents in a tree are an interesting biological event—especially if they can't be reached with the pruning shears.

Mischievous Moths
Masquerade as Hummingbirds

What's not to like about hummingbirds? These beautiful little birds are one of the true miracles of nature. They zoom about our flowers in search of nectar. They are more than happy to accept a free handout at hummingbird feeders. And much to our delight, they stage spectacular aerial battles in quarrels over food or territory.

There are moths that look and behave much like hummingbirds. These insects do an excellent job of mimicking hummingbirds—such a good job, in fact, that they are called hummingbird moths!

However, that is not the only common name used for these bird mimics. They are also called hawk moths. This bird name is apparently based on their ability to fly rapidly. Some of these moths can fly more than 30 miles per hour.

Another common name for these insects is sphinx moth. This name is derived from the behavior of the larval stage of the insects. When disturbed, the larvae sometimes rear up, presenting a visual image that resembles that famous statue in the Egyptian desert.

Most of us are probably more familiar with hummingbird moths when they are in the immature stage rather than in the adult stage. Caterpillars of hummingbird moths are known as hornworms. There are a lot of species of hornworms, and all of them have a single horn on their rear ends.

One of the most common is the tomato hornworm. This is a large, green worm that feeds on tomato plants. Most tomato hornworms are discovered when a gardener notices that the leaves on tomato plants have disappeared. Those leaves have been devoured by the hornworms.

Once the hornworm reaches its mature size of about 3 inches in length, it crawls down from the plant and digs into the soil. Once in the soil, the caterpillar fashions a cell, complete with cement-like walls. There, the caterpillar turns into the pupal stage. The pupa is brown or black in color and is sometimes discovered by gardeners when they plow the soil. The pupae that develop in the fall spend the winter snug in their soil cells.

The following spring, pupae that have survived the chill of winter change once again. This time, the miracle of insect metamorphosis results in the adult insect—the hummingbird moth. The moths then show up sipping nectar from flowers.

Flowers that are attractive to hummingbirds are also attractive to their namesake moths. The long beak of the hummingbird allows it to extract nectar from flowers while hovering in front of the blossom. The hummingbird moth feeds in the same manner, also using a long feeding tube. But the moth coils up its mouthparts when not in use.

Some of the hummingbird moths are about the same size as hummingbirds. Since the two creatures also share similar coloring and behavior, it is easy to see why they are sometimes confused with each other.

There are many species of hummingbirds, and they range in size and color patterns. So it is with hummingbird moths. These moths also feed on various food plants as caterpillars. The tomato hornworm commonly feeds on tomato, as the name suggests, but in addition, it also feeds on tobacco and potatoes. There is a paw paw sphinx, an elm sphinx, a sage sphinx, and a cypress sphinx, and they are all hummingbird moths. The catalpa sphinx larvae, as you guessed, feed on catalpa, and make good fishing bait.

One unusual group of hummingbird moths lacks scales between the veins on the wings and is called clearwing hummingbird moths. Several have yellow and black coloring and mimic bumble bees. Many groups of insects are good bee mimics, but only within the hornworms do we find mimics of both the birds and the bees!

Butterflies have made frequent appearances in pop music. Mariah Carey named an album "Butterfly," and the band Crazy Town had a hit single with that title. "Butterfly Kisses," which means the act of fluttering eyelashes quickly against someone's cheek, have also been mentioned by plenty of musicians, including in songs by U2, the Barenaked Ladies, and Tim McGraw.

Hymenoptera

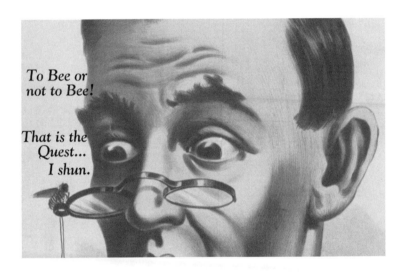

The insect order Hymenoptera includes ants, bees, wasps, and sawflies. Hymenoptera wings are clear and membranous. But not all Hymenoptera possess wings. Many ants and even a few wasps are wingless. Hymenoptera vary in size from tiny parasitic wasps that develop in insect eggs to wasps that exceed two inches in length.

Of all of the insect orders this one probably contains more species directly beneficial to humans than any other. One way that we benefit from Hymenoptera is that some insects in this order, primarily the bees, are plant pollinators. The insect and plant pollination connection is essential for fruit production in many plants. It has been estimated that as much as 30 percent of the human diet, the fruits and vegetables, result from insect pollination.

Another food item that indirectly results from the intimate relationship between insect and flower is honey. Honey bees accept a nectar bribe offered by flowers and use it as the raw material for honey production. The bee, in exchange for the nectar, provides pollen transportation from flower to flower. Honey bees consume honey as needed but store excess as a food resource for use during times when nectar is unavailable in the field.

Humans and other animals love sweets and have for eons robbed honey bees of their stored honey. Humans maintain honey bee colonies in a practice called apiculture for the purpose of producing honey and wax. In 2004 over 184 million pounds of honey were harvested from honey bee colonies in the United States. Honey production is a labor-intensive endeavor for the bees. Bees have to fly an average of 55,000 miles to produce a pound of honey. Consequently the U.S. honey production in 2004 required the

equivalent of 406,425,702 bee trips around the earth at the equator. That is a lot of miles to produce enough excess honey to satisfy the human sweet tooth.

Many wasps are parasites or predators of other insects and spiders. Wasps that attack the insects that we call pests are considered beneficial organisms. Well over a thousand species of parasitic wasps play important roles in what has become known as biological control. Biological control is where one living organism is used to control the populations of organisms that are pests. Some of these wasps are produced commercially and can be purchased for use in insect control.

A few species of Hymenoptera are themselves pests. Ants show up in our homes and at our picnics in search of food, and their presence annoys us. Ant mounds in our lawns and fields can be a problem. Carpenter ants are so named because they sometimes hollow out wood to construct a nest chamber. If that happens to be in the structure of our home, we are not happy.

The ability of some Hymenoptera to sting in defense of themselves and their nest means that these insects can cause injury to humans. Most bee and wasp stings cause temporary swelling and isolated pain. But there are some people who are allergic to bee or wasp venom and for them a sting could be fatal.

The order Hymenoptera includes three groups with social structure: all of the ants, some bees, and some wasps. All termites are also social insects, but they belong to the order Isoptera. Social insects exhibit three defining characteristics. All have castes, such as queen, drone, and worker; the adults feed the immatures; and overlapping generations are present in the nest. Some scientists maintain that the social structure among insects is one highest evolved forms of animal life.

As far as we know, all males of Hymenoptera result from unfertilized eggs. That means that males within this order possess only one set of
chromosomes. In other words, male bees, wasps, and ants have a mother
but no father. And females have a father but no paternal grandfather. Kind of
reminds me of that old song by Ray Stevens—"I Am My Own Grandpa!" But
that is another story.

In its entire lifetime, the average worker bee produces 1/12 teaspoon of honey.

"The Ants Go Marching Two by Two, Hurrah, Hurrah"

Ants are very common insects. So common, that many scientists consider ants to be the most successful of all insects. In fact, if you just count number of individuals, ants outnumber most other terrestrial animals.

Ants live in colonies that vary greatly in size, from a few dozen to thousands of individuals. Ants are social insects, and colonies have at least three castes. These castes are queens, males and workers. The workers are sterile, wingless females and are the ants most people encounter, since they look for food outside of the nest.

Male and female ants have wings used for mating flights. The queen also uses her wings to fly to new nest locations. Once the queen establishes a new nest, she chews off her wings. They are of no value in a new home. The wing muscles are absorbed to provide energy for the queen to start laying eggs. In addition, the bulky wings just get in the way in the close confines of a nest. The queen, like a human bride, finds that her wedding dress is not functional attire for raising a family.

Ants exhibit a wide range of lifestyles. Some are carnivores. They feed on the flesh of other animals, either living or dead. Army ants exhibit such feeding behavior. These ants are mostly tropical. They are nomadic and travel in distinct armies. Like raiding armies on the move, no animal life is safe as they sweep across the countryside.

The carnivorous habit of ants includes feeding on other species of ants. This leads to furious battles between nests of ants. One battle was recorded by Henry David Thoreau in his story "The Battle of the Ants." In this story, Thoreau chronicles a battle between a group of black ants and smaller red ants. He appropriately compares the fighting to legendary battles in Greek mythology.

Many species of ants feed on sap, nectar, or honeydew. All of these substances are high in sugar and are prized by ants as a food. It is for this reason that some species of ants actually farm aphids. These ants collect honeydew produced by the aphids. Aphids are sometimes called ant's cows. The ants protect the aphids from predators and even move their "cows" to greener pastures when necessary. A few species of ants also store aphid eggs in their nests during the winter.

There are ants known as harvester ants. The name is based on the fact that these ants harvest seeds, which are stored in the nest as a food resource. Other ants actually produce food. These ants are known as leaf cutter ants. The ants harvest leaves and bring them into their nest. They do not feed on the leaves, though. The ants start growing fungus on the leaves in chambers known as fungus gardens. The fungus is consumed as food.

One interesting food storage habit of ants involves using living ants as storage tanks. These ants are known as honey ants. Some individual ants serve as reservoirs for the honeydew collected by other workers. These ants, known as repletes, hang from the roofs of the nest chambers filled with honeydew. When other ants need honeydew, they stroke the mandibles of the replete, which prompts the living storage tank to regurgitate some of the sweet liquid.

A well-publicized habit of ants is that some species utilize other species of ants as slaves. A few species of ants are entirely dependent on slaves. The process varies some, but frequently involves a queen moving into another species of ant nest and killing the resident queen. The nest workers then adopt the new queen and take up the duty of rearing her offspring. These workers then make raids on other ant nests, where they kill the workers and bring back the pupae to rear as slaves.

So when the ants go marching two by two, as the old children's song recounts, those ants are on a mission. It could be to harvest seeds, milk cows, battle with neighbors or even capture slaves. Who said insects sometimes behave like humans?

What Would a Picnic Be without Ants?

Summer is the season for picnics. Picnics are defined as pleasure parties with food provided by the participants. Generally, a lot of food! Officially, picnics are held outdoors.

There are many kinds of picnics. Picnics come in all shapes and sizes. Some are sponsored by companies, political parties or service organizations. These picnics are frequently adorned with banners and accompanied by speeches and photo ops. Other picnics are family reunions where distant cousins get reacquainted or meet for the first time. Still other picnics are private affairs with one family and a picnic basket packed with goodies.

So popular is the idea of a picnic that we even have special tables just for such things. Parks have shelters and provide outdoor grills for cooking to accommodate picnic groups.

Regardless of the type or location of the event, one thing that all picnics have in common is that insects will show up to pester the human participants. Flies and yellow jackets buzz around, picnic beetles land in the salad, mosquitoes look to extract a blood meal from the human participants and ants march across the table.

Ants are so common at picnics that some fabric designers have even included ant images on the red-and-white checkered fabric that has come to symbolize picnic tablecloths.

Ants are a very common and widespread group of insects. They are, in the opinion of many entomologists, the most successful of all insect groups.

As individuals, ants probably outnumber all other animals in terrestrial habitats.

All ants are social insects that live in colonies in nests. This means that individual ants must leave the nest and collect food for the colony. Food habits of ants vary widely. Some ants are carnivores that feed on living animals. In this case, the food is frequently of the insect type, including other ants. Some ants are herbivores and feed on plant material. Still others are omnivores and feed on a combination of plant and animal food.

So why do ants show up at our picnics? The same reason that humans show up—food!

But how do ants find the picnic? It works this way. Certain worker ants in the colony are foragers. This means the ants leave the nest in search of food. In order to find their way back to the nest, the foragers will mark the path with a chemical called formic acid. The foragers just wander around until they encounter a food source. Then they haul some of the food back to the nest. This is accomplished by carrying a piece in their mandibles or swallowing a morsel. The latter approach requires that the ants regurgitate when they get back to the nest. Either way, workers are recruited to help bring the food home.

When ants find a good food source, they quickly bring others to the location to harvest the food. It is the ant equivalent of the saying, "Making hay while the sun shines." Each ant that goes to the food source remarks the trail. So the trail to the food is constantly trod by worker ants on their way to the food or coming back to the nest.

The trail will not always be the most direct route from the nest to the food. The trail reflects the path the first worker took as she was searching for a food source. But each of the ants will follow the same trail. It would appear

that ants are wasting energy by not taking the most direct route to the food source.

So what if ants aren't as efficient as we sometimes make them out to be? If ants are headed to a picnic, the scenic route might be preferred. After all, it is the atmosphere that makes a picnic fun. There are more efficient ways to have a meal.

Locusts can eat their own weight in food in a day. A human eats his own body weight in about half a year.

Warrior Ants on the March

It is the stuff horror movies are made of. Hordes of seemingly mindless individuals terrorizing every living thing in their path. Unafraid of humans or any technology that the human mind can conceive, these creatures use fearsome jaws to wreak havoc on all they encounter.

"They" are warrior ants, sometimes called army or driver ants. No wild-eyed scriptwriter has to dream up such a movie tale. It already exists!

Warrior ants live in the semitropical regions of South America and Africa, but unlike most other ants, they do not have a permanent home. Warrior ants form bivouacs from which they raid surrounding areas in search of plunder. Or they go on marches during which it is said they consume all of the animal refuse in their way. During such frenzied marches, they will not hesitate to attack all kinds of vertebrates, including human beings.

Many are the tales of encounters with the warrior ants. Dr. Albert Schweitzer had to conquer the warrior ants, among other things, as he developed his hospital in Africa. Of particular interest to Schweitzer was the chicken house. At the onset of a warrior ant invasion, Schweitzer would jump out of bed and run to open the chicken house door. According to the famous doctor, "Shut in, they would inevitably be the prey of the ants, which creep into their mouths and nostrils until they are suffocated, and then devour them, so that in a short time nothing is left but their white bones."

Another well-known doctor who devoted his life to Africa also records encounters of the unpleasant kind with warrior ants. This doctor was none other than the one who prompted the journalist Sir Henry Stanley to exclaim upon finding him living on Lake Tanganyika, "Dr. Livingstone, I presume."

Dr. David Livingstone recorded in his diary that the camp "suffered a furious attack at midnight from driver ants." In an attempt to keep the ants away, Livingstone's men lighted grass fires. In his last diary entry for the day, he wrote: "We put hot ashes on the defiant hordes.'" Apparently to no avail, because the good doctor noted that he had suffered bites so numerous that he resembled a person who had smallpox.

In some parts of Africa, criminals were punished a century or more ago by binding their hands and feet and laying them in the path of an ant army. François Coillard, a missionary in Africa, reported that under such circumstances, "in a surprisingly short time the writhing victim will have been changed into a skeleton of clean and polished bones that will make the trained anatomist envious."

Over time, such observations of warrior ants have no doubt helped give credence to mothers' admonitions to fidgety children: "You're wiggling around like you have ants in your pants!"

Insect Carpenters

Carpenter bees and carpenter ants. These insects don't carry hammers or saws, or belong to a local carpenter's union. However, their wood work creates few friends in the human world.

Bee and ant carpenters build their homes by hollowing out wood. This is accomplished by using their strong mandibles. They literally chew out a new dwelling. In the woods this home building activity is largely unnoticed by humans. However, when either of these insects decides to make their home in our homes, we are less than hospitable.

These insect carpenters can weaken the structure of a house by building their domiciles. So we call them pests and try to get rid of them.

Carpenter bees resemble bumble bees. However, the carpenter bee is nearly black, while the bumble bee has yellow markings. Also, bumble bees are fuzzy, while carpenter bees are slick. They excavate a nesting burrow in exposed timbers like rafters and porch-railings. The entry hole to the burrow is normally upward into the wood for about an inch. The burrow then turns and runs with the grain of the wood. The female bee makes cells which are filled with pollen and nectar and separated with wood pulp. One larva lives in each cell.

Much of the concern about carpenter bees is due to the habit of the males flying around the nest area. Males cannot sting, and females, unlike bumble bees, will not defend their nest. They only will sting if mishandled.

Carpenter ants are large and black. They can be either winged or wingless. The presence of carpenter ants in a home does not mean they are nesting there. These ants will look for food away from their nest and will often search a human dwelling for something to eat.

Carpenter ants, like human carpenters, leave sawdust as evidence of their work. A pile of sawdust on the carpet may indicate that these insect carpenters have constructed their new home in yours. If this is the case, it is probably wise to do something about the ants. Their nests can weaken the structure of our homes.

Most homeowners find it necessary from time to time to have carpentry work done. But not the kind provided by carpenter bees or carpenter ants.

A Bee or Not a Bee—
That Is the Stinging Question!

When it comes to bees, almost everyone has an opinion. Most of those opinions are on the negative side. And for good reason--bees can sting! Consequently, many people associate bees with stings. And stings, or the potential for stings, are not on most folks' "top 10" list of favorite things.

In general, a bee sting is painful and results in swelling and discomfort in the affected area for a few days. However, some people are allergic to bee venom, and, for them, a sting might be fatal.

If you happen to get stung by an insect, say "ouch" or "pickle" or some other appropriate descriptive term, and then remove the stinger if it is still in your skin. It is a good idea to wash the sting area as soon as possible since infection sometimes results from a sting. Put ice on the sting to reduce pain and swelling.

Be alert to symptoms other than pain, itching and a small area of redness and swelling. Symptoms that might indicate an allergic reaction are large areas of swelling, abnormal breathing, tightness in throat or chest, dizziness, hives, fainting, nausea or vomiting, or persistent pain or swelling. If such symptoms occur, medical attention is advised.

Of course, avoiding bee stings is a good policy, and something most of us try to do. Under the category of the obvious is that the best way to avoid bee stings is to avoid bees! But in the summertime, that is easier said than done.

Not all stinging insects are bees. In fact, some of the most common insects that sting are wasps and hornets.

One such hornet that stings is known as a yellow jacket. These yellow and black insects resemble honey bees in size and color. So when yellow jackets frequent picnics, ball games and fairs in August and September in search of food, many people incorrectly call them bees.

It doesn't matter if a stinging insect is a bee or a wasp; the venom is injected into the victim through a modified ovipositor. Ovipositors are egg-laying devices of insects. Egg production is a function of female insects so that means only female insects have the equipment to sting. Hence, all stinging insects are females.

The stinger on a honey bee is a barbed affair, sort of like a harpoon. Those barbs will prevent the stinger from being withdrawn from the skin of a mammal. That means that when a honey bee stings a human, it generally hurts the bee worse than the human. You see, when the bee tries to fly away from its victim, it literally rips its rear end off. And it dies. Only honey bees have barbed stingers. Bumble bees, wasps and hornets lack barbs on their stingers and can infect venom multiple times.

So why do bees, wasps and hornets sting? To defend themselves or their colony, that's why. So the best way to avoid bee stings is to not antagonize female bees. Don't bother their nests, and don't swat at them when they are flying around you or the flowers in the garden. Stinging insects don't go out looking for a fight, but, if you make them mad, you are likely to pay the price!

Not All Bees and Wasps Sting

The first thing that comes to most people's minds when they hear the word bee or wasp is sting! Yes, the ability to sting is one of the notable characteristics of these insects. Not all bees and wasps sting, though. In fact, most species of bees and wasps never sting humans. However, those that do provide the reputation for all of the rest.

Those bees and wasps that sting do so with a modified ovipositor. Ovipositors are structures that female insects use to lay eggs. Mostly insects use their ovipositors to insert eggs into such things as soil or plant tissue. Some wasps have ovipositors that are used to insert their eggs into other insects, where their babies feed on the innards of the victim. These wasps are called parasites, and when they attack pest insects we call them biological control agents.

Some of the parasitic wasps also have glands that produce poison used to paralyze prey insects. Wasps that use their stingers in this way are said to sting offensively. They sting to provide food for their offspring.

At some point in the past, some wasps probably started to use their sting and their poison gland to protect themselves and their nests. Such stinging is called defensive stinging. These are the wasps that will sting humans. Bees that sting are all defensive stingers. No bees sting to provide food for their offspring.

So which bees and wasps sting and which don't? Of the hundreds of species of bees and wasps, only a very few will sting humans. Those that sting are generally the largest of these insects. Some of the stinging wasps include most of the so-called paper wasps. These insects fashion their nests from chewed wood, hence their name. They include bald-faced hornets, yellow jackets, and the paper wasps that many times construct their nests under the eaves or windowsills of a house. In general, the mud daubers do not sting, except in the rare instance where someone will pick one up in their hand.

Among the bees, the most common stingers are the bumble bees and the honey bees. Another common stinging bee is a small metallic-colored bee called a sweat bee. Named after its habit of gathering sweat, it will sting when it is touched, such as with a hand or a fold of clothing. Such a sting normally prompts a response from the human a slap that just adds insult to injury, since the stinging bee has normally already flown away.

Even among the bee and wasp species that sting, not all individuals are able to do so. You see, stinging among insects is a female thing. It takes a modified ovipositor to sting, and males don't have the proper equipment. Among most of the bees and wasps, a high percentage of individuals are females and can sting. However, half of the well-known bumble bees are male. So if you happen to sit on a bumble bee, you have a 50/50 chance of not getting stung!

The Yellow Jackets Are Coming

Fall—the harvest season. That time of the year when pumpkins lie in golden contrast to the fading green vines of their nurturing plants. When sun-ripened apples are turned into sweet must under the unrelentless crunch of a cider mill. When the quiet serenity of a backwoods picnic or suburban cookout is suddenly broken with a blood-curdling scream: "yellow jackets!!"

Yes, folks everywhere slightly modify Paul Revere's now-famous warning of Revolutionary War times. "The yellow jackets are coming, the yellow jackets are coming" is an oft-repeated warning of close encounters of the insect kind.

Yellow jackets are common, ground-nesting, social wasps. In the spring, a mated female emerges from her overwintering site and establishes an underground nest in an abandoned rodent burrow. There she begins the task of rearing young wasps. Early growth of the colony is slow, because the queen does all of the work. However, by midsummer other wasps have been produced. These workers take over the duties of food finding, larval care and defense of the nest. By late fall, some yellow jacket nests may contain as many as 3,000 workers.

Immature yellow jackets are fed meat, mostly in the form of arthropods captured by workers. In the fall, when prey species become scarce, the yellow jackets become scavengers. They can be found around garbage cans and are frequent visitors to picnics. That, of course, causes great concern to the humans, who are reluctant to share the feast with six-legged visitors, especially those armed with a sting.

In general, yellow jackets do not sting except in defense of their nest or when physically abused. Therefore, remaining calm is the best policy when faced with a yellow jacket intent on tearing meat from your bologna sandwich or skating on the ice cube in your cola. Aggressive behavior normally prompts a like response on the part of the yellow jacket, and in most cases, the insect will be victorious. If the yellow jacket nests in lawns are a continual problem, they can normally be eliminated by finding the hole to the nest and treating with an insecticide during the night. However, such activities can be hazardous to your health, because yellow jackets will not stand idly by while their home is being destroyed.

In most instances, folks are well-advised to leave the nests alone. Yellow jackets are beneficial because of the insects they destroy, and winter will solve the problem for another year. Besides, who wants to be guilty of stirring up a hornet's nest?

Spring in the Colonies

Spring is an exciting time of year in temperate regions of the earth. It is a time of birth and growth—a time of renewal. It is a busy time when humans and other animals and plants prepare to take advantage of the impending growing season.

Nowhere, though, is life more frantic in the spring than in the colonies—the honey bee colonies, that is. With the lengthening days and the promise of summer flowers, the colony is abuzz with activity. The queen has begun to lay eggs, and production of summer workers has begun. The current workers are, you might say, busy as bees.

A key to the success of the colony is to have high numbers of workers available during the summer months. These workers not only tend to duties within the hive, but also must collect nectar for processing into honey. To the colony of honey bees, it is essential to make honey when the sun shines. A good store of honey is necessary for survival during winters in temperate regions of the world.

Honey bees are like human industrial organizations in that workers progress through steps the longer they have been on the job. For instance, the oldest workers in the colony are the bees seen on flowers in the field. Before these forager bees get to wing their way over hill and dale in search of nectar and pollen, they must serve the equivalent of an apprenticeship beginning with the task of cell cleaning. That job lasts about three days.

The young worker bee moves from cleaning woman to nursemaid. During the next 10 days she will feed larvae. First the old larvae, then the younger ones and even the queen. From this task she gets promoted to the pollen and nectar storage detail. Next, she is called on to secrete wax, and finally to guard and ventilate the hive. All of this has taken approximately three weeks, and the worker is ready to move from hive bee to field bee.

The field bees will live about another three weeks during the busy days of the summer, when the flowers are full of nectar. During this time they will make thousands of trips to the field and literally work themselves to death.

Unlike human factories that can hire additional workers for peak production times, the honey factories have to plan ahead and produce the workers for those busy times. The honey bee colony is really busy in the spring time so there will be a lot of bees to be busy in the good ol' summertime.

Insect Masons Build Little Mud Houses

In June and July, many people notice that their homes are being adorned with mud. Not the proverbial mud tossed around by politicians, but mud brought in by a group of wasps known appropriately as mud daubers.

These insects get their names because they construct mud homes for their offspring. They place their mud structures in protected places. Bridges, abandoned buildings, barns, garages, and porches and eaves of human dwellings are prime real estate for these insect mud masons.

Mud daubers acquire the raw material for their nest at the ground level. They frequently can be found crawling around a mud hole picking up soil in their jaws. Once they have acquired a load of the raw material, a ball of wet soil, they fly to the job site. There the soil, mixed with insect saliva, is used to fashion the nest.

Like humans, the mud daubers build their homes in different shapes. The organ-pipe mud dauber produces a series of side-by-side tubes that look like the pipes of a musical organ. Each pipe is fashioned of strips of mud that just happen to be the width of the wasp's jaws. The color of the nest sometimes changes as the pipe gets longer. This reflects the color of the soil used, and the wasp may change the site of soil collection as the nest grows.

Other mud daubers take time to smooth the surface of the nest. In this case, the ridges of soil evident in the organ-pipe mud dauber nest are not evident. The smoothing activity is similar to producing a stucco human home where the masonry material is smoothed over the outer surface.

A few mud daubers really live up to their name. They appear to just deposit the jawsful of mud in a haphazard way on a pile. The resultant home looks like a handful of mud thrown against a wall.

These mud homes have a cavity inside that is filled with food for the immature wasps. This food is often spiders. So once a mud dauber has a room constructed of sufficient size, the room is filled with enough spiders to feed the offspring during their immature life. An egg is then placed in the cell, as the room is called, and the mother then seals the cell with a partition of mud.

Mud daubers are generally black wasps with orange markings or bluish-black in color. As a general rule, these wasps crawl around in a nervous fashion as they work. They move fast and flip their wings and abdomen frequently. Unlike the paper wasps, they almost never sting humans.

Another characteristic of mud daubers is that they sing while they work. When they're working inside a nest under construction, you can hear them making a buzzing sound. To some people that buzzing sound is a happy sound. It is the sound of a mud dauber building a house for her children—children she will never see because when they emerge next June, she will be gone. But she did what every good mother does for her children—provided a good home and lots of food!

Bees and Flowers Play the Pollination Game

Flowers and bees! Bees and flowers! No matter how you look at it, you really can't separate the two. In the natural order of things, bees depend on flowers and flowers depend on bees.

This flower and bee thing is what scientists call mutualism. It is a partnership where both participants benefit from the association. So how does it work?

Like a lot of things in nature, it all boils down to reproduction. One of the most common reproductive approaches used by plants is based on seeds. Production of seeds begins when pollen from the male parts of a plant contacts the female parts of a plant. Then some X-rated things happen involving pollen tubes, styles and other plant parts. Ultimately, a seed develops.

If both the male and female parts are from the same plant, the process is called self-pollination. If the male and female parts are from different plants, that is called cross-pollination. Cross-pollination is good since it results in gene mixing and produces what has come to be known as hybrid vigor in the offspring.

Plants, unlike animals, can't go searching for mates. Instead, plants just send their pollen in search of mates. Send may not be the correct word. The pollen has to be transported. Sometimes the pollen is carried by the wind. Other times pollen is carried by insects.

Several groups of insects transport pollen from flower to flower. Beetles, butterflies and wasps have been shown to carry pollen. However, one group of insects, the bees, are the premier pollen bearers of the insect world. Unlike other insects that transport pollen by accident, the bees do so intentionally.

Bees and flowers actively play the pollination game. The process is one of the miracles of nature. But neither the flowers nor the bees play the game just for fun. We're talking serious biological business here. The flower has a job that needs to be done. It needs pollen transported. The bee needs food to feed its family. This is the biological version of "Let's Make a Deal!"

Flowers produce a fine quality food called nectar. This sweet substance is utilized by many insects. Unlike other insects, bees have developed a process to refine and store nectar as honey.

So what we have here is a classic economics problem. Flowers have a raw material that is needed by bees. But economics teachers warn that you can't stay in business if you sell products below costs. This is true of flowers. So nectar is bartered. Bees provide a pollen transport service in exchange for nectar. In order to ensure that the bee carries out its part of the deal, the flower does not provide a full load of nectar for a bee. Each flower provides just enough nectar to entice the bee to feed. It must go to other flowers to complete the load. When that happens, pollen is transferred from flower to flower.

But in the rough-and-tumble world of business and nature, it is not enough to provide a wonderful raw material like nectar. The plant has found that it pays to advertise! Plants do so with flowers. The flowers function to attract the bees to the plant. Once there, the bee makes its way to the nectar distribution center. On the way, it crawls by the pollen-dusting facility where grains of pollen stick to hairs on its body.

So what if the bee seems to have been tricked into carrying the pollen for the plant? Remember, "All's fair in love and war!" And in pollination, apparently.

Killer on the Loose

There's a killer on the loose! But neither the FBI nor the local police departments are concerned. You see, this killer is of the insect kind. It's a cicada killer.

Some people are frightened by these wasps, quite understandably. Cicada killers are one of the largest wasps in North America. These rusty brown insects with yellow stripes range from 1 to 1½ inches in length. That size wasp, one is to assume, has a good-sized stinger! Indeed, the female is said to be able to deliver a serious sting.

For the most part, people's fear of cicada killers is unfounded. These wasps reserve most of their stinging activity for—you guessed it—cicadas. The adult wasps catch cicadas. Often the catch is made while both are on the wing. The cicada killer then stings its victim, a process that paralyzes the cicada. Before the cicada is paralyzed, it squeals loudly. It makes quite a sight—this B-52 of the wasp world headed toward home with a squealing cicada in its legs.

The cicada killer uses the cicada to feed its young. The wasp first digs a hole in the ground. At the end of the hole, 6 inches or more in depth, the mother-to-be places one or more cicadas. She then lays an egg, which hatches in two to three days.

The newly hatched larvae begin to feed. The adult wasp has guaranteed a fresh food supply for her young by paralyzing the cicada. Not just any cicada, mind you, but a particular species, the dog day cicada. The cicada is immobilized, but remains alive. The larvae keep the cicadas alive by selective feeding. They destroy nonessential parts of the host first, leaving the vital organs until the final stages of feeding.

By fall the larvae have completed development. They then pupate and hibernate until the following summer, when a new crop of cicada killers begin to ply their trade.

It is the wasp's behavior in the vicinity of the nesting sites that frightens people. The wasp buzzes around, hovering menacingly, as it checks out intruders. Fortunately, it seldom resorts to warfare as a means of protecting the nest.

When in the vicinity of the nesting grounds of cicada killers, the best approach is to keep your cool. And it might be prudent to minimize noises similar to those made by a cicada!

Dance, Honey Bee, Dance

Dancing, according to my trusty dictionary, is a patterned succession of movements. That's the reason we humans take dance lessons. We sometimes have to learn the steps.

Dances can be done alone or with others. Many human dances are performed to music. Some humans have even been known to dance in the rain. What was the deal with Ginger Rogers and Fred Astaire anyway?

Human dances have long been performed to convey messages. Many dances of Native Americans were supplications for good crops or preparation for war.

Humans aren't the only dancers in the animal world. Birds and insects perform dances to attract the opposite sex. So, for that matter, do humans! Dog owners also recognize an apparent dance for joy by their canines. None probably as accomplished as the ear-spinning, toe-waggling aerial pirouettes by everyone's favorite cartoon pooch, Snoopy!

When it comes to dancing, no animal, human or otherwise, does it like the honey bees. Honey bees are famous for their dances. Honey bee dances are an important communication tool. That is why the honey bee dance is sometimes called the language of the bees.

How does the dance work? The primary function of the honey bee dance is to communicate location of a nectar source. To do this, a returning foraging bee will do one of two dances on the comb in the hive. The first is called a round dance, because the path the bee follows is round. This indicates that the nectar source is less than 100 meters from the hive. In other words, the bee is telling other field bees to go out of the hive and look around within 100 meters for the flowers.

The more complex, and more famous, dance is called the waggle dance. In this instance, the dancing bee waggles her abdomen in the straight part of a figure-eight dance pattern. The direction of the waggle part of the dance communicates direction relative to the sun. For instance, if the dance is away from gravity, up on the comb, the nectar source is toward the sun.

The abdomen wiggling is accompanied by sound pulses. The number of pulses is used to convey to other bees the distance to the flowers. A short flight means less pulses, a longer flight more. So, for increasing distances, the waggle runs take longer.

These dances are designed to recruit new foragers to the food source. On a first trip, the bees follow the route outlined in the dance. Once they find the food, based on the route they learned, they improvise and make return trips, according to landmarks along the way.

Returning bees do, however, dance to communicate with other bees, and their dance is based on the direction of the sun. They even correct for the movement of the sun across the sky, even though research has shown that sun position is not of much importance to returning foragers.

Another dance that loaded, returning bees do is called a tremble dance. In honey bee colonies, the loaded bees are unloaded by hive bees. When the incoming nectar exceeds the ability of the hive bees to unload the foragers, the field bees begin to back up.

When this happens, the loaded bees do what is a distinctive shaking motion and create a vibration on the comb. This stops other bees from doing their field dances until all incoming bees are unloaded. In human terms, the

bee is stamping her feet and saying something like "Stop that waggling and get over here and take this nectar!" Even dancing bees can get a little surly when they have to wait in line for the dance floor.

The dehydrated larvae of the African chironomid *Polypedilum vanderplanki* are able to withstand exposure to liquid helium (−270° C) for up to 5 minutes with a 100% survival rate.

Hornet Artisans

By November, Mother Nature has normally completed her age-old seasonal ritual: the shedding of leaves. Each year as winter approaches, deciduous trees in temperate climates everywhere drop their excess baggage. Those leaves, like lovers scorned, float aimlessly earthward.

But the annual departure of the leaves reveals more than just bare, nurturing limbs. Hornet's nests, hidden from view by summer foliage, suddenly stand naked against the winter sky. Hornet artisans build and maintain their homes for months. Then in the fall, like the leaves that had concealed it, the hornet's nest is left to the wiles of nature. It will soon be gone.

Bald-faced hornets—whose name comes from the white spots between their eyes—are engineers of the highest order. They construct their globe-shaped nests from a paper-like material. The hornets collect wood from any available source, and by chewing and mixing it with saliva, they produce the nest material. Because these insects frequently use different sources of wood, the nest may appear multicolored.

As the summer progresses, the nest is enlarged to accommodate a growing family. By the summer's end, many nests are basketball-sized or larger.

Bald-faced hornets pack a powerful sting, and few things are madder than a mad hornet! Most hornets are quite docile, at least when away from their nests. However, they are willing, even anxious, to sting in defense of the home.

Hornets feed protein to their young. They are active hunters and can frequently be found around homes in pursuit of flies. They have even been known to land on people after mistaking a button or spot on clothing for a food item.

Hornets are beneficial because they prey on pest insects, but some people might say the greatest benefit of bald-faced hornets is the decorative value of their nests. Indeed, many hornet nests have ended up hanging over the mantel of the fireplace. Procuring such a decoration from the wild carries with it the inherent risk of introducing a few hornets into the house.

Each fall bald-faced hornet queens mate and seek shelter in woods to overwinter. The next spring, the queen starts the process over. The remaining workers stay with the nest until they are killed by freezing temperatures.

Of course, the rather fragile nest must be maintained constantly, and a nest will not last long when exposed to seasonal winds and marauding animals. Therefore, a good nest for decoration must be procured after the tenants are deceased but before it is blown to pieces. That, my friends, is where the rub—or rather the sting—comes in.

Honey Bees Become Beasts of Burden

We have long lauded the honey bee as one of the most useful insects to humans. After all, these hard-working arthropods provide all kinds of products. Honey for our biscuits. Wax for our candles and fine furniture. Pollen for our health food diets. And royal jelly for anything that ails us! Honey bees also carry pollen from plant to plant—a process that ensures the availability of an abundance of fruits and vegetables to tempt our pallet.

But now researchers at Cornell University have come up with yet another way that bees can work for us. Joseph Kovach, an associate professor of entomology at Ohio State University, reported that bees can carry a biological fungicide to flowers of strawberry plants. Kovach and his associates have made the honey bees into miniature spray planes.

Here's how it works. The researchers put pans of a biological fungicide, a microorganism that controls gray mold, in front of hives. The field bees headed out for a load of pollen or nectar walked through the material and picked it up on their feet. When the bees got to the flowers, hopefully strawberry flowers, some of the biological fungicide wiped off on the blossom. The fungicide then prevented the disease gray mold on the strawberries.

The system worked so well that the bee-borne treatment resulted in more than 25 percent heavier berries than comparative treatments applied with a sprayer. This was achieved with 50 percent less fungicide.

The willing worker bees seemed not to mind that they were toting stuff from the hive. They are accustomed to carrying material. But field bees generally carry things into the hive.

This is not the first time that honey bees have carried things in the name of science. Researchers have glued microtransmitters to honey bee backs in efforts to determine whether or not these insects fly in bee lines. They, as it turns out, do not!

Honey bees have been loaded down with weights to determine just how much they can carry while on the wing. It turns out a lot—at least by airplane standards. A honey bee has been shown to carry as much as 70 milligrams of nectar. That is 85 percent of the average weight of a bee. A typical load of nectar for a bee is 40 milligrams. No airplanes can come close to carrying such a payload.

You can imagine that the fertile minds of scientists have conjured up all kinds of ideas about things that honey bees might carry, for instance miniature TV cameras. Just think of all of the places that a honey bee is capable of visiting with a camera on its back.

CIA types have, no doubt, given some serious thought to using this insect beast of burden in some clandestine camera work. But there is a problem. Honey bees are independent sorts and go where they please, normally in search of something useful to the hive. So, unless there is a flower garden in the area under surveillance, it is unlikely that a bee will visit.

Bees aren't homing pigeons. In fact, they aren't homing anything. They go on a mission and then fly back to where they started their trip. You can't carry a honey bee away and expect it to come home.

And that is just fine with most people. As long as the bees keep bringing nectar home to their hive, it's a sweeter world for all of us.

Honey Bees Live in Nests

The insects that we know as honey bees have existed on earth since the Eocene geological period. That's about 50 million years, or many, many millennia. All the while, the industrious bees produced honey and stored it as food. A few thousand years ago, humans began to satisfy their sweet tooth by eating honey produced by the bees.

Humans procured honey either by hunting for bee nests in the wild or practicing honey bee agriculture. The latter we know as bee keeping.

According to their nesting habits, honey bees can be divided into two groups. The first type of honey bee builds single-comb nests in the open. These outdoor-nesting bees can produce massive combs, sometimes 6 feet across and more than 3 feet high. Such nests can contain more than 100 pounds of honey.

These are the types of bee nests that are collected by the honey hunters of Nepal. The nests are suspended from rocks high on cliffs and are protected from most predators. However, the honey hunters hang suspended by ropes on the face of the cliff while dislodging the nests into bamboo baskets. Just the kind of exciting activity that makes a good National Geographic TV special!

The single-comb, outdoor-nesting bees are common in tropical regions of the world where low winter temperatures do not exist. Some 5 million years ago, a second group of honey bees appeared.

These honey bees are called cavity-nesting species, and they build a nest with a number of parallel combs. The cavity-nesting honey bees were able to survive in temperate regions of the world.

Not only do these bees benefit from the protection provided by the

cavity where they nest, but they also "cluster." During cold weather, the bees form a ball, and the mass provides insulation and concentrates body heat in the center of the ball to keep the insects from freezing.

Cavity-nesting bees look for natural nest sites in the wild. They are found in caves, rock hollows or holes in trees. In modern settings, honey bees are sometimes found in wall spaces of buildings or even in the attic of homes.

Historically, finding honey bee nests in forests was one way that people in the United States procured honey. Many times the so-called bee trees were cut down and the bees smoked out before the honey-filled combs were collected. This resulted in destruction of the colony.

In parts of northern Europe, some people practiced what has become known as tree beekeeping. This activity involved preserving the nest in the hollow tree so that honey could be harvested on an annual basis.

Eventually, humans began to keep bees. The earliest hives were just sections of a hollow tree cut for the purpose of providing a nesting site. Another early nesting site provided by humans was an inverted basket made of woven plant stems. These wicker bee baskets are called skeps. Coiled straw was eventually more commonly used for skeps than wicker. Today, either straw or wicker skeps are popular decorations for gardens.

Eventually, wooden boxes were constructed for bee nests. Such boxes varied in size and shape. Some were highly decorated and looked like miniature houses, complete with sloping roofs. Others were hexagonal in shape. Some were merely rectangular or square boxes. This is the general shape of hives used by most beekeepers today.

The shape of the hives used to house bees is for the convenience of the beekeepers. To bees, the appearance of their home is of no importance. All they need is protection from the weather and a space to store honey.

Diptera

The order Diptera has around 124,000 described species. Insects of this order are known as flies and are among the most recognizable of insects. Flies zoom around throughout the spring, summer, and fall, with occasional aerial excursions even on warm winter days.

There is a lot of structural diversity among flies, but many have large compound eyes and all have only two wings. Most types of insects have four wings as adults, and a few adult insects, such as fleas and lice, do not have wings at all. But only the flies have two wings; that is the basis for the order name Diptera (Di = two and ptera = wing).

Some insects called flies are not classified in the order Diptera. Butterflies, dragonflies, sawflies, and caddisflies have "fly" in the name but are not really flies. You can tell by the way the name is written. It is one word. A real fly would have the name written as two words, as is the case with the house fly.

Flies have only half as many wings as most other flying insects but, as most of us have noticed, it doesn't seem to hinder their ability to fly. The hind wings of Diptera are reduced to small knobbed structures called halteres. Halteres function as a balancing and guidance system for the insect while in flight. Indeed, flies cannot fly if their halteres are removed.

Most flies are relatively small soft-bodied insects. All flies have antennae, but in many species, like the house fly, the antennae are short and inconspicuous. In other Diptera, such as mosquitoes and midges, the antennae are long and visible.

Flies live in all kinds of habitats and feed on all kinds of food. Immature

flies are legless and in many species are known as maggots. Many Diptera adults, like mosquitoes, are blood feeders and are notorious pests of humans. The Diptera transmit a number of human diseases, including malaria and sleeping sickness, and the death and misery these diseases bring have had a major impact on the history of humankind throughout the ages.

In spite of the nasty things that flies do to us, they play important functions in the environment. Many recycle dead plant and animal material. Almost all Diptera are major food items for insect-eating animals, including birds, fish, frogs, and other insects. This is an ecological activity in which most of us would just as soon not participate. Remember the tale about the old woman who swallowed a fly?

Doggers of Civilization

Of the world's pest insects, none are more prominent than flies. These "two-winged" insects have been called "doggers of civilization." And for good reason.

Of the ten plagues of ancient Egypt, two were flies. Fly-borne diseases are said to have hastened the decline of the ancient civilizations of Athens and Rome. Sleeping sickness, a disease transmitted by the tsetse fly, long delayed the civilizing of Africa.

The ancient Semitic people recognized a deity known as Beelzebub, Lord of the Flies. It might have been wishful thinking, but these people thought that Beelzebub would defend them against flies. The Philistines of the era apparently couldn't depend on Beelzebub. They appointed a fly control officer. No one knows how this first government-sponsored program for insect control worked out.

Songwriters have recognized the importance of flies as pests. "The Blue Tail Fly" is about a species of horse fly that has a vicious bite. The song became so popular that it was number one on radio's hit parade of songs in the late 1940s.

Many sayings exist that relate to flies and fly behavior. Most people prefer not to have "a fly in the soup," but other lessons can be learned through the less common sayings of our ancestors. For example, a lesson on the value of even the smallest thing, "Every fly has its shadow"; on hard work, "Flies are busiest about lean horses"; on common sense, "Even flies won't light

on a boiling pot"; on overdoing it, "Cover yourself with honey, and the flies will have at you"; on watching what you say, "No fly gets into a shut mouth"; and on watching your step, "If the fly flies, the frog goes not supperless to bed."

Flies also have a reputation as weather predictors. Flies collect on the screen door just before a storm. Flies, it is said, "bite sore when there is a good chance for rain."

Modern civilization is still fighting flies. Flies are annoying us and stealing our blood and that of our animals, and we can't entirely stop them. To be sure, we have window screens, flypaper, and flyswatters. We even have insecticides, but we still have flies.

The most common of all flies is the house fly. Even its scientific name—*Musca domestica*—indicates how closely it lives with mankind. While the house fly can't bite with its sponging mouthparts, it has been implicated in disease transmission. These flies can carry germs that cause dysentery, diarrhea, and food poisoning.

The house fly, in spite of all its imperfections, appears polite. The little beast always cleans every one of its six feet before tromping around in the mashed potatoes and gravy on your plate.

Flies Have Families, Too

Most people are not surprised to learn that there are lots of flies in this world. In fact, the insect order Diptera, the flies, is one of the largest orders of insects. Flies can be found almost everywhere.

All flies are not the same, and to help keep track, scientists divide these insects into groups called families. Sort of like the Hatfields, the McCoys, and the Smiths and Browns. Most of these scientific names are larger than the insects themselves. For instance, one family of flies is named Lonchopteridae and includes flies less than five millimeters in length. It would take at least a dozen of these little flies placed end to end to be as long as their scientific name!

Many flies also have common names—names that are a bit more understandable to most people. The Lonchopteridae are also called spear-winged flies because their wings are somewhat pointed at the end.

Sometimes common names, like spear-winged flies, are descriptive of the insect. For instance, the small-headed flies have unusually small heads, even for flies. On the other hand, one might assume the big-headed flies think they are socially better than other flies, but they actually have really big heads for flies. There are also thick-headed flies, which might be a little difficult to teach new tricks. There are long-legged flies, stilt-legged flies, and stalk-eyed flies. Some flies are called picture-winged flies because it looks as if someone has attempted to paint their wings.

There are flies called dance flies because they have the habit of doing

a rather elaborate mating dance. It just might be that some flies overdid this dancing a bit, because one group is known as the flat-footed flies.

Some flies are known by their general appearance, such as the bee flies, which resemble bees, and louse flies, which look more like lice than flies. Snipe flies have a head with a long proboscis that faintly resembles that long-beaked bird called a snipe. Rust flies are so named not because they were left out in the rain, but because they are the color of oxidized steel.

Other flies take their common names from where they are found. Such is the case with the stable fly and the house fly. Flower-loving flies can be found around, you guessed it, flowers. Bat flies are associated with bats, and face flies hang around the faces of cattle. Deer flies feed on deer and other mammals, and horse flies are pests of horses.

Soldier flies and robber flies are named more for their behavior than their looks. Seaweed flies, marsh flies, and small dung flies have names that describe their habitat or hangouts.

A fly is not just a fly any more than all humans are Joneses or Walgenmuths. Some people really don't care to know the difference, but then the same can probably be said for a biting fly that looks at a human as just another warm-blooded meal!

April Showers, May Flowers, and Mosquito Blood Banks

April showers bring May flowers—or so the old saying goes. But there is a downside to those spring rainfalls. They are also partially responsible for the summer's mosquito crop.

Those night-flying, blood-thirsty mosquitoes live as immatures in standing water. So rains that provide water to nourish the spring blossoms also fill potholes and low-lying areas in woods and back yards that become breeding sites for mosquitoes.

There are lots of different kinds of mosquitoes. More than 100 species live in the United States. They occur from Alaska to the Gulf Coast states; they thrive from the marshes of the eastern part of this country to the deserts of Arizona. And all of them have at least two things in common: female mosquitoes need a blood meal to produce eggs, and their immatures live in water.

As a general rule, the female mosquito lays her eggs during May and June. She lays them one at a time or in groups of 100 to 400 on the surface of the water. In one to three days, the eggs hatch into what is called a wriggler. The wriggler gets its name from the motion it makes as it moves through the water.

Wriggler mosquitoes do not get oxygen from the water, as do other insects that live in the water. Rather, they are air breathers. They get air through a miniature snorkel, a siphon, that is attached to the rear end of the insect. The wriggler breathes by coming to the surface and sticking its snorkel

through the surface of the water. The fact that the wriggler has to get air from the surface has led to a method of control in which the water surface is covered with a film of oil. The oil prevents the young mosquito from getting air, and it suffocates.

Mosquito wrigglers feed on microscopic plants, and in a week to ten days they molt into the pupal stage. In this stage, they are shaped like commas and stay near the surface of the water with breathing tube in contact with the air. When disturbed, they will leave the surface in a sort of tumbling motion and are sometimes called tumblers.

In two to three days the tumbler becomes an adult mosquito. The skin of the tumbler splits down the back, and the winged adult climbs onto the skin and uses it as a float until it is ready to fly.

The newly emerged adults use their wings to continue the population of mosquitoes. The males fly off to find females, and the females, once mated, fly to find a host to supply a blood meal. That is the part of the mosquito's life cycle that most of us dislike. That is when we are asked to donate a little blood so the female mosquito can produce another generation of eggs. Most of us would just as soon not contribute, but the mosquito doesn't ask. She just helps herself!

Little Fruit Flies Cause Big Disturbance

Fruit flies are not one of the largest insects in the world. But they are one of the best known. These little flies get their name from their association with fruit. There are two groups of fruit flies.

One group, which belongs to the scientific family known as Tephritidae, has immatures that feed on a variety of plant materials. Some that feed on fruits have become major agricultural pests. Two of the worst pests of this group are the Mediterranean fruit fly and the apple maggot.

The Mediterranean fruit fly, sometimes called the medfly, attacks over 250 kinds of fruits and nuts. The adult fly lays eggs under the skin of fruit. The eggs hatch into headless maggots that bore into the fruit pulp. The feeding destroys the fruit and may introduce bacteria or fungi that will cause the fruit to rot.

The medfly is native to South Africa, but like a lot of pest insects it has managed to find its way to other parts of the world. It is found throughout Europe, Central and South America, Australia, and Hawaii. It has appeared in Florida and California several times. Each time the medfly was found in these states, it has been eradicated with attractants and chemical controls.

Unlike the medfly, the apple maggot is a native insect. It probably originally fed on hawthorn before apples were grown in North America. It is a major pest of apples and must be controlled in most apple production areas. While the medfly and apple maggot are major pests, most people don't

worry a great deal about these insects. There are other fruit flies, however, which are encountered by most people on a regular basis.

These fruit flies are classified as Drosophilidae and are known as Drosophilia. They are also known as pomace flies and are generally seen near decaying fruit or other vegetation. Breweries and vinegar factories frequently harbor populations of these insects, which give rise to another common name, vinegar flies.

Most of us will see these pesky fruit flies when we have ripe fruit around the house. Fruit fly populations are especially high during the fall when a high volume of fruits and vegetables begin to rot on the tree or vine. Getting rid of these little flies is a matter of getting rid of the ripe fruits and vegetables. My grandmother would just leave a couple of slices of melon or tomato in a bowl sitting in the kitchen overnight. The next morning she would place a dishtowel over the bowl and carry it and the captured flies outside!

Annoying though they may be, Drosophilia fruit flies have played an important place in scientific discovery. These insects are easy to produce in the laboratory and have been used to unlock the secrets of genetics. In fact, scientists have mapped the entire DNA code of the fruit fly *Drosophilia melanogaster*. Who cares, you ask? Well, humans and fruit flies share many genes, and many of the genes identified in the fruit flies are the same as genes linked to diseases in humans. So the secret to a healthier life for humans might be found in the lowly fruit fly.

In the meantime, I'll let the scientists raise their fruit flies if they want. I'll continue to swat those that try to share my slice of ripe breakfast muskmelon!

Menacing Mosquitoes Are
Vamps, Tramps, and Scamps

Very few insects are as despised as are mosquitoes. And for good reason. They bite! But there is more to the mosquito problem than the bite. By transmitting disease organisms, mosquitoes have caused more human suffering than any other group of insects!

So it is easy to see why humankind doesn't love mosquitoes. And with the spread of the West Nile fever across the U.S., most people have become even more aware of the mosquito menace.

How have creatures as small and fragile as mosquitoes wreaked so much havoc on humans? The fact that they feed on blood is the key. In addition, as species they're tough. Mosquitoes have been around for eons and they seem to be everywhere on the earth.

What's with this blood feeding habit anyway? Blood is necessary for the female mosquito to complete development of her eggs. So the mosquito that bites is a female. There are some exceptions to the "only the female bites" rule. In a few species the male seeks a blood meal. Also on rare occasions males of other species, individuals with a sexual identity crisis, also feast on blood.

These insect vamps practice their skills on many kinds of animals. If an animal has blood it is fair game for these winged, blood-seeking hypodermic needles. Birds, mammals, and even snakes and lizards unwillingly donate blood in support of mosquito reproduction.

How does this insect phlebotomist go about her business of blood collection? She is endowed with the perfect equipment for such a job. The mosquito's mouth consists of several parts. There are two tubes, one for sucking up blood the other for delivering a liquid to keep the blood from clotting. Two pairs of sharp knives called stylets surround the tubes. Stylets are used to cut the skin.

Once an incision is made, the tips of the mouthparts are inserted. If a blood vessel has been cut the blood is sucked up. If not, the mosquito moves the tips of the mouthparts around in the incision trying to hit a vessel. If a blood vessel is not contacted she will drill another hole.

After the female imbibes enough blood to suit her needs, over two times her own weight, she quietly leaves the blood donor. She will land on the nearest vertical surface and begin to digest the meal. The water is removed from the blood and excreted in mosquito urine. She stores the remaining good stuff in her body.

A bloodthirsty female mosquito discovers her victim based on several clues. First there is odor. Mosquito antennae have detectors for carbon dioxide and lactic acid. We produce both of these chemicals when we breathe. The many-faceted mosquito eyes are good at detecting movement. So any motion will help a mosquito find her victim. Finally with the thoughts of your blood dancing in her head the vamp focuses on the hottest part of your body. That would likely be a patch of bare skin!

It is the feeding of the mosquito that creates problems for humans. For many of us the problem is merely some itching that is a direct result of the anticoagulant chemicals injected to prevent blood clotting.

But the biggest concern associated with the bite of a mosquito is not a mere itch. The real problem is when the mosquito is infected with an organism that can cause disease. Such organisms include viruses, bacteria, roundworms and protozoans. Mosquito-borne diseases are a major world health problem and are estimated to kill more than 2 million people each year.

Historically, diseases carried by mosquito vectors have done much more than just cause human illness and death. These diseases have had a major impact on the history of the world. One such disease is yellow fever.

Yellow fever is caused by a virus and was introduced into the New World from Africa along with its vector, the mosquito *Aedes aegypti*. Yellow fever has long been associated with seaports, including Havana, Boston, New York, and New Orleans.

It is this disease that was largely responsible for the failure of the French to complete construction of the Panama Canal. The United States took over the project following the departure of the French. By controlling the mosquito populations through sanitation, the threat of yellow fever was significantly reduced and the United States succeeded in the project.

And now the virus that causes West Nile fever has reached our shores. The virus resides in birds. It can be transmitted to humans by a mosquito that has taken a blood meal from an infected bird. While the risk of acquiring West Nile virus is very low, the presence of the virus in an area means that we should reduce the potential for mosquito bites as much as possible. After all, that mosquito vamp threatening to sample your blood might have acquired her previous meal from some infected bird down the road!

Deer Flies Aren't Dear Flies

One of the real insect menaces of late spring and early summer is the deer fly. These fairly common flies are rather stout-bodied. Most are about the size of, or slightly larger than, house flies. They frequently have brightly colored or iridescent eyes.

While some people might not have taken a good look at these insects, most of us have at one time or another had contact with a deer fly. Female deer flies feed on the blood of mammals. Today cattle and horses are frequently attacked. Deer are also a prime target, and that is the basis for the common name given to this type of biting fly.

Deer flies are normally encountered near streams or marshy areas because the immature flies develop in water or saturated soil. However, the adult flies can fly miles, so they're sometimes found far from breeding sites. The flies are attracted to natural light and are frequently found in windows, where they congregate after flying into a garage or house.

These flies are not gentle feeders, and that is why they are such an annoyance to any animal that is a meal target. The adult female extracts blood from a victim by first inflicting a deep gash with the blade-like portion of her mouthparts. Then she laps the flowing blood with the spongy part of her mouth. Of course, the bite is painful, and the bitten animal normally reacts by stomping, tossing its head, or even running.

Deer flies also attempt to feed upon humans who venture into their habitat. The insect on its feeding forays normally dive bombs the victim. Deer flies seem to target the human head and sometimes get caught in a person's hair. All of this is very annoying, especially when several hungry flies are intent on extracting blood at the same time.

Humans besieged by deer flies frequently resort to a slapping or flailing behavior in an attempt to avoid becoming a meal for these blood-thirsty insects. Sometimes we even try to outrun the flies. Fat chance! Flies can cruise at nearly 30 miles per hour and seem to enjoy such a chase. Most human and deer fly encounters result in at least one fly managing to get in a bite. When that happens to humans, we can really sympathize with their animal victims. These insects are anything but "dear" flies!

Ants cannot chew their food, they move their jaws sideways, like scissors, to obtain the juices from the food.

The Case of the Headless Horse Fly

Horse flies are biting insects. They feed on the blood of their victims. The insect has a blade-like part of its mouth that it uses to slash the skin of an animal. The fly then sponges up the blood that emerges.

Horse flies feed on mammals, including horses, cattle and, occasionally, humans. The bite of the horse fly is painful; consequently, food targets of this insect are not willing participants. Horses and cows stomp and run. Humans swat and sometimes catch the offending insect.

When a horse fly is captured, the more sadistic among us have, at times, destroyed the insect by decapitation—an obvious effort to get even with an insect that would dare dine upon us.

When a horse fly is beheaded, a strange thing sometimes happens. The headless horse fly flies away! Now that is the stuff of horror movies or Halloween tales.

But how does a horse fly manage to fly without its head? Good question. Scientists who study such things really don't know either. However, there is much that is known about insect flight.

For instance, many insects fly when they sense danger. A horse fly, even a headless one, can be provoked to take flight by touching it. The touch displaces sensory hairs on the insect's body. A nerve impulse is transmitted from the hair, and the insect responds by taking flight. Obviously, that action does not require the presence of the insect brain in the case of the headless horse fly. The brain was, after all, removed with the head.

Some insects, including flies, take flight when their feet are no longer in contact with a surface. That response is a tarsal reflex action. It works in the same way as a reflex action in our knee when tapped with a mallet. The information is gathered by the feet, or tarsi, but is not transferred to the brain. The information goes directly to the wings. So if the headless fly is lifted off the surface, it begins flight activity, and away it goes.

How a headless insect maintains orientation in flight is another question that comes to mind. In general, insects make constant corrections for forces that tend to disrupt the stability during flight. These destabilizing forces are measured by hairs on the insect body and wingbeat patterns modified by the central nervous system.

Flies even have flight stabilizing organs. Called halteres, these organs replace the back pair of wings of flies and work like gyroscopes to monitor forces working on the insect during flight. The information appears to be processed in the central nervous system, not the brain.

What all of this means is that a headless horse fly does not need its brain to fly. And so for a few seconds, it can take off and fly—even approaching a horse fly's top speed of twenty-two miles per hour. But without a head, the horse fly cannot see where it is going and will crash into the first thing in its way. That is because the eyes of the insect are used to determine the flight path. Literally, the headless insect is flying blind.

Or if nothing gets in the way, the headless flying fly does a dive into the earth when its systems begin to break down because of the lack of a brain. In the meantime, though, it is a sight to see a headless horse fly zooming off into the wild blue yonder. Especially if it has just taken a bite out of your ankle!

Why Mosquitoes Buzz in People's Ears

The soft whine of a mosquito has been known to keep people awake all night. The wing beat frequency of mosquitoes, sometimes 300 beats per second, produces a sound that has come to be recognized as a warning of things to come—a little bloodletting by a mosquito!

The sound of mosquitoes and our reaction to it are summed up in a West African folktale. The tale is retold in a delightful children's book entitled *Why Mosquitoes Buzz in People's Ears*. The tale begins with an iguana who disbelieved a mosquito's story that "I saw a farmer digging yams that were almost as big as I am." Rather than listen to such nonsense, the iguana stuck sticks in his ears.

The iguana's inability to hear precipitated a series of abnormal behaviors by other animals, ultimately causing the death of a baby owl. The mother owl was so distraught that she would no longer hoot, a process that was necessary to bring the sun up. The result was that the day did not come. The animal king, the lion, called all the animals to a council fire to discuss the situation. At the town meeting the animals ultimately concluded that everything was the result of the lie that the mosquito had told.

Of course the animals demanded that the mosquito be punished. This action satisfied the owl, who resumed her duty of calling up the sun each day. The mosquito, however, remains a felon. To this day she is plagued by a guilty conscience and goes about whining in people's ears whether or not people are still mad at her.

When she asks, according to the tale, she gets an honest answer: she gets smashed! Sometimes actions speak louder than words.

Other Orders

The Lord
of the Locust

Classification of things is an important aspect of science. The system of classification in natural history begins with a broad division known as kingdom. Accordingly all things fall into one of three kingdoms—mineral, plant, or animal. Things in all kingdoms are further divided into groups based on similarity of characteristics. The animal kingdom is divided into about a dozen groups called phyla. Insects fall into the phylum (singular of phyla) Arthropoda.

Arthropods have segmented bodies, paired appendages, and an exoskeleton. Millipedes, centipedes, crayfish, lobsters, shrimp, scorpions, ticks, mites, spiders, and the insects are all arthropods. The phylum Arthropoda is divided into classes. Insects fall into the class Insecta (some scientists use the name Hexapoda for this class). Classes are further divided into orders.

Order names, like many names used in scientific classification, are frequently based on Greek roots. For instance, many insect order names end in ptera, the Greek root for "wing." Butterflies and moths are classified as Lepidoptera, the scale-wing insects. Beetles are the sheath-wing insects, the Coleoptera. The Diptera are the two-wing insects that are generally known as flies.

Entomologists disagree about the number of orders of insects but the number is from 26–31, depending on the way that the insects are grouped. For instance cockroaches, mantids, and walking sticks have been grouped in the order Dictyoptera (as in this book) but sometimes are divided into three orders, Blattaria, Mantodea, and Phasmida respectively.

In terms of number of species that have been named, the largest order of the class Insecta is Coleoptera, with about 300,000 species. Next is Diptera,

with 120,000 species. There are 112,000 species of Lepidoptera, and 108,000 species of Hymenoptera. These are the four largest insect orders according to number of species, and understandably the most frequently encountered and recognized by most people.

Other insect orders do not have as many species but some have species that make them well-known. For instance, most people know about cockroaches in the order Dictyoptera because of the pest status of a few cockroach species. Termites, the Isoptera, are also known because of their habit of eating the wood in our structures. The pest nature of some of the Hemiptera and Homoptera also keeps them on the minds of many people.

Mantids are also widely recognized because of their size, their interesting biology, and their status as a beneficial insect in lawns and gardens. Some of the Neuroptera, the lacewings, also are predators on other insects and are known as biocontrol agents.

The dragonflies and damselflies in the order Odonata are also insect predators and are easily observed flying about streams and ponds, where their immatures live in the water.

Many singing insects are included among the grasshoppers, katydids, and crickets. So while we may not visually encounter as many individuals in this order as in some insect orders, we do notice their sound. It appears that insect orders with many species attract our attention, but so do those orders that have species that are large, damaging, or noisy.

By Any Name, a Cockroach Is Still a Cockroach (Dictyoptera)

Cockroaches would not be on most people's favorite-insect list. In fact, cockroaches might just be among the most hated insects in the world.

Why the cockroach has reached the lofty peak as the most hated among insects is not entirely clear. P. B. Cornwell, in his book *The Cockroach,* suggests that even though cockroaches are potential carriers of disease, their pest status is primarily due to aesthetic abhorrence. We consider them loathsome intruders into our abodes. They run fast and unpredictably. They produce a characteristic odor and foul anything they contact with their excrement, including our food. Their numbers can increase dramatically.

The scientific names for cockroaches give little indication of their pest status. Some such names are based on Blatta, the Latin word for this insect. For instance, *Blatta orientalis* and *Blattella germanica.* The word cockroach itself is probably derived from the Spanish word "cucaracha"; however, one of the earliest names for this insect was "lucifuga," an apparent reference to its habit of shunning the light.

Of all the insects in the world, no group has more local names than the cockroach. The Oriental cockroach has been called black beetle in England. This is an apparent reference to its color and the English habit of calling any insect that crawls a beetle. It also has been called the mill beetle and the black clock, probably because it appeared at dusk. In the United States this cockroach is frequently called a waterbug, in reference to the damp areas of a home where it is frequently found.

The German cockroach, one of the most common cockroaches found in our homes, is known by a variety of names including steam bug and shiner. It is called the Croton bug in the eastern United States. This name is based on large increases in its populations in New York about the time the Croton aquaduct was constructed.

The American cockroach is known in the southeastern United States as the palmetto bug because it hides in the bark of palmetto trees. On ships, the American roach is called the Bombay canary.

One interesting pattern of naming cockroaches is to name them for groups of people who are disliked. In northern Germany the cockroach is called "Schwabe," a term used to describe southern Germans. In southern Germany these insects are popularly known as "Preusse," after the northern Germans. In the former East Germany the local name was "Russe," after the Russians, and in West Germany they were called "Franzose," after the French. In Nova Scotia a cockroach is called Yankee settler.

I don't suppose naming the despicable cockroach after a group of people you don't like would be politically correct, but it does get a message across.

Pious Frauds of the Insect World (Dictyoptera)

One insect everyone seems to like is the praying mantis. Few insects are held in such high regard by humans. The reason is that mantids feed on other arthropods. And by most human standards, anything that eats other insects is good!

Mantids also exhibit some interesting biological characteristics. Unlike most insects, they can turn their heads. This allows mantids to gauge the distance of potential meals so that they don't attempt to catch prey outside their reach.

Some female mantids also make a meal of their mate. The male mantid is decapitated by the female—a behavior that some people regard as, well, interesting!

So we like mantids. So much so that some people think that it is against the law to kill them. While no such law exists, there is no reason to kill mantids, since they don't harm us, our pets, our plants, or our possessions.

But there is more to this insect than meets the eye of the average beholder. Mantids are, as Odgen Nash called them, "pseudo-saintly" bugs. They are "pious frauds," according to nature writer Harold Bastin in his book *Freaks and Marvels of Insect Life.*

So what is the story of this widely recognized insect? Most mantids are protectively colored. Their color allows them to blend into their environment. Such camouflage is of survival value to the insect.

First, mantids do not chase down and catch their prey. They wait for the potential meal to crawl or fly within range of their forelegs. So the camouflage means that the prey does not see the mantid until it is too late. Secondly, mantids themselves are prey for birds, lizards, and other enemies. So the protective color serves to hide the mantid from mantid-eaters.

A good example of how this works is exhibited by the common European praying mantis, which has two distinct color forms. One form is green, the other brown. The green form is found on living green foliage, while the brown form hangs around dead and decaying leaves.

The Italian naturalist A. P. di Cesnola was curious about colored mantids, so he tethered some green mantids on brown foliage and some brown mantids on green foliage and vice versa. He discovered that most of the green mantids on the brown background and the brown mantids on the green background were either destroyed by predators or starved to death.

On the other hand, when the background colors were reversed the mantids did just fine. The moral of the story is that mantids do better when they don't stand out!

This mantid masquerade is even more highly developed by a Malayan mantis that resembles a pink orchid. So close is the resemblance of the insect to the flower that bees and butterflies mistake the insect for the flower and land on it. Once this happens, the mantid turns the fooled insect into a meal. Mantid deception is even enhanced when the insect periodically sways from side to side as if being caressed by a gentle breeze.

While we humans think praying mantids are wonderful insects, it is obvious the insect is no saint. So maybe we ought to change the name from praying mantid to preying mantid!

Water Striders Use Tension to Stay Afloat (Hemiptera)

Water striders are appropriately named. These insects are able to glide over the surface of the water with the greatest of ease. Being able to walk on water is a miracle of sorts in the animal world—so much so that some people refer to water striders as "Jesus bugs."

Not many creatures in the animal world actually live on the water surface, as do these insect striders. Some ducks and geese spend much of their life on water; so do some seagulls and terns. These birds are floaters. They are animal boats. Waterproof feathers form the bird equivalent of a hull. The creature displaces enough water to keep it on the surface.

Water striders, though, are different. They manage to stay on the surface by using the surface tension of the water to hold them up. Remember in grammar school how, with great care, you were able to float a needle on the surface of the water in a glass? The secret was to not break the surface tension of the water. Otherwise, the needle did a miniature version of the Titanic and headed to the bottom of the glass.

So how does this insect strider manage to pull off this miracle? It has the right stuff. Its insect equivalent of toes, called tarsae, are covered with very fine hairs that are difficult to wet. These nonwetting hairs do not break the tension of the water, so the insect floats, or skates, on the surface.

Those who have observed water striders closely notice that the insect appears to have only four legs. All adult insects have six legs, and the water strider is no different. However, this insect uses its front legs, which are smaller than the four used as pontoons, for capturing prey—in much the same way that praying mantids use their front legs. The front legs do not contact the water, so only four legs are obvious to the casual observer.

Water striders float over the surface of the water in search of their food, which consists of small insects. Any hapless insect that falls into the water and stays afloat for a moment is potential food for these predators.

In general, water striders are found in protected areas of freshwater ponds or streams where the water is quiet. However, they can be seen riding the waves in fast-moving streams as well. One species lives on the surface of the ocean and can be found many miles from shore. It is one of the few insects that has any association with ocean water.

These insects lay their eggs on floating plant material. The newly hatched young skate over the water like their parents. Neither young nor adults can live under water, and if they sink, they drown. Occasionally this happens. When the tiny hairs on their tarsae become wet, the insect cannot float and must climb up off the water to dry out.

Winged and wingless individuals occur in most species of water striders. It is the winged individuals that are found in unexpected places at times—for instance, in the birdbath.

What happens to water striders when the water where they are living dries up? Well, they might fly away or, in the case of a larger spring or pond, they just crawl under a rock or in the mud and hibernate until the water returns. After all, it's hard to stride on the water if there is none!

Insect Groupies (Hemiptera)

Every rock and movie star has groupies. So do athletes. On the golf links Arnie Palmer had his army. These human hangers-on are common around the rich and famous.

Even insects have groupies—at least they hang around in groups. One such insect groupie is the boxelder bug. No famous individual attracts these bugs. They just hang around for the warmth of it. You see, they gather in groups to absorb the rays of the sun.

Each fall, as the season turns cooler, boxelder bugs begin to congregate in great numbers. These groups of strikingly marked red and black insects can be found everywhere—on trunks of trees, on porches, on walls, and even on sidewalks. Often the presence of large numbers of boxelder bugs causes a great deal of concern among humans in the vicinity.

Such concern is unwarranted. Boxelder bugs can neither sting nor bite. They do not harm food or clothing. However, they do seek protection during the winter months in the sheltered places. Sometimes these places are our homes. However, most homeowners take a fairly dim view of sharing their domicile with a bunch of insect groupies.

Homeowners have been known to take drastic measures to eliminate boxelder bugs. One such method is to attempt to burn the bugs. This approach generally involves a homemade torch on a pole. But the secondary effects of such an effort can be a problem—for instance, singed hair from falling pieces of disintegrating torch. And we cannot forget the possibility of an emergency run by the fire department if the fire gets a little out of hand!

A better approach is to spray a common insecticide. Another way to reduce the problem is to eliminate boxelder trees in the vicinity of the house. These insects feed primarily on the seeds of the boxelder tree, but they also consume seeds of ash trees. Removal of the food source—in this case, the trees—will reduce the population to low levels.

Boxelder bugs characteristically have a disagreeable odor and taste. This is well known to people who have accidentally encountered this insect. Such a bad taste, a fact advertised by its bright color, keeps the insect from being eaten by insect predators.

Boxelder bugs aren't called boxelder bugs by everyone. In parts of the Midwest, these insects are known as democrats, an unusual name compared to other common names of insects. I was once told that the name democrat reflected the habits of these insects: they always hang around in little groups and raise a stink. Of course, the fellow who mentioned that was in fact a Republican!

Even insects aren't immune to politics.

The Treetops Are Alive with the Sounds of Cicadas (Homoptera)

As has been the case for many millennia, summer brings the sound of cicadas. Cicadas are members of the insect order Homoptera. This order includes plant hoppers, leaf hoppers, whiteflies, scale insects, and aphids.

Most people recognize these insects as pests. And many Homoptera do damage plants by feeding on plant sap and sometimes transmitting plant diseases.

Homoptera generally are small insects. Cicadas are an exception. They range in size from one to two inches in length.

Cicadas are well known because of their sound production. Two organs on the abdomen are used to create sounds. Each organ includes a membrane and a ribbed structure called a tymbal. When the tymbal is vibrated by strong muscles, the "song" is produced and amplified by the membrane.

Cicada songs are produced only by males. The male sings to attract the female of the species. Each type of cicada has a specific song, but to humans, most of the songs can be described as a buzz. When many cicadas are singing in unison, the buzz can become quite annoying—and loud! So loud that some folks have described the music as a deafening racket.

When the first European settlers arrived in North America, they encountered great emergences of cicadas and called them locusts, the name commonly used in other parts of the world for migratory grasshoppers. As a result, in the United States, we frequently refer to cicadas as locusts.

By either name, locust or cicada, it has an unusual life cycle. The adult female lays eggs in slits under the bark of the twigs of trees. The eggs hatch and the young cicada drops to the ground, where it crawls into the soil. In the soil, it feeds on the roots of trees.

After its immature stage is complete, the cicada crawls out of the soil, mostly during nighttime hours. From there, it climbs up tree trunks, sides of houses or fence posts where it attaches and emerges from its immature skin. The skin, called a shell by many people, is left for children to collect.

Cicadas, depending on species, spend anywhere from 1 to 17 years underground during the immature stage. The species with the 17-year life cycle are known as periodical cicadas. There are also periodical cicadas with a 13-year life cycle. Either way, the periodical cicadas have the longest life cycle of any insect, except the termite queens of Africa.

The emergences of periodical cicadas sometimes results in millions of the adults present at the same time. Under these circumstances, the trees are literally alive with flying and singing insects. Native Americans were well aware of the singing cicadas. But these resourceful people enjoyed more than the song of the insect. Many Native Americans collected cicadas as they emerged from the soil, roasted them over a fire and ate them. For them, it was a delicacy complete with dinner music, provided by the delicacy!

Aphids Sometimes Called Plant Lice (Homoptera)

Almost anyone who has tried to grow a plant has come into contact with insects known as aphids. Aphids are small insects that average about a tenth of an inch in length. But what these insects lack in size they make up for in numbers, and that is why they become pests.

It was the great numbers of these insects that prompted Erasmus Darwin, grandfather of Charles Darwin, back in the 1700s to describe them as a "prolific tribe." Prolific they are. Aphids are masters of reproduction. One aphid can become thousands in a few weeks.

How does that work? Most populations are made up only of females. These females reproduce parthenogenetically—that is, reproduction without the benefit of mating. Aphid females have cut out the "middleman" in the reproductive process, an approach to procreation that is sure to warm the cockles of the hearts of radical feminists everywhere!

Eliminating males in the reproductive process saves time. No searching for mates or courtship required. In addition, these mavens of insect reproduction give birth to living young. In a matter of days, these young themselves give birth. It all adds up to a rapid increase in aphid numbers—what ecologists call a population explosion.

Aphids are what some entomologists call sap suckers. These insects use their piercing-sucking mouthparts to remove sap from host plants. The aphid digests some of the sap, but most is eliminated. The waste material is very high in sugar and is known as honeydew.

Because of the sugar content, honeydew is collected by ants as food. That's why ants are frequently found in association with aphids. In fact, the relationship is so common that aphids have been called ants' cows. In some instances, ants actually protect the aphids from predators. In the case of corn root aphids, ants carry the aphids to new plants. This activity would be akin to a shepherd moving sheep to a new pasture.

Aphids are very successful in spite of a number of predators and parasites that feed on them. The parasites include tiny wasps called braconids and chalcids. These little wasps go unnoticed by most people because they are so small. However, owners of plants may sometimes find brown aphid carcasses with a round hole in the back. Those are aphids that were consumed by parasites.

Predators also eat aphids. Three of the most common include the ladybugs, the lacewings and larvae of some syrphid flies. Both adult and immature ladybugs eat aphids. The same is true of lacewings. Immature lacewings are such voracious consumers of aphids they are called aphid lions! Syrphid flies are also called hover flies and, because they are colored like bees, incorrectly called sweat bees by many people.

Aphids are very specific to the type of plant on which they feed. But there are lots of species of aphids, so most plants can have aphids. The aphid names reflect food plants. We have alfalfa aphids, apple aphids, and bean, cabbage, cotton, corn leaf, and green peach aphids. There are also plum and melon aphids and rose and spiraea aphids. There are also aphids with the name walnut, pear, clover, spinach, and turnip. Hey, these little insects are everywhere. No wonder some people call them lice.

Leafhoppers by the Zillions (Homoptera)

Leafhoppers seem to be everywhere during the summer. These small insects, measuring only millimeters in length, can be found on almost all types of plants.

They feed by taking sap from leaves. Their feeding pattern plus their habit of jumping when disturbed has given them the name "leafhoppers."

Many leafhoppers have a single generation a year and spend the winter in the adult or egg stage. Some are seasonal invaders, coming into the Midwestern states in the spring as passengers on a spring weather system.

Leafhoppers are significant pests of plants. Damage is caused in several ways, including stress due to the loss of sap. Some species injure plants by laying eggs in twigs. Other species are vectors of major plant diseases, including potato yellow dwarf and corn stunt.

One of the most common pests of this group of insects is the potato leafhopper. Though it is a pest of potatoes, it also feeds on alfalfa and soybeans. When the potato leafhopper attacks alfalfa, its saliva produces a toxic effect, causing the leaves to turn yellow in a V-shaped pattern.

You don't have to grow potatoes or alfalfa to consider the potato leafhopper a pest. This insect invades our homes much too frequently. The potato leafhopper really doesn't want to be a house guest. It just happens to be an insect that cannot stay away from lighted windows.

The potato leafhopper is so small that it can go through window screens in search of the nearest light fixture. By the next morning, leafhopper carcasses are strewn like fallen infantrymen across counter tops, in light fixtures, and on window sills.

Home owners who have enlisted bug zappers in their personal battle-of-the-bugs will find that their prized device has claimed leafhoppers by the buckets full. Still, many leafhoppers manage to find their way into the house. In the battle with insects, we humans have come to realize that numbers can sometimes overcome the most modern devices.

More human deaths have been attributed to fleas than all the wars ever fought. As carriers of the bubonic plague, fleas were responsible for killing one-third of the population of Europe in the fourteenth century.

Termites: Nature's Wood Destruction Crew (Isoptera)

In nature's grand scheme of things, insects have many jobs—for example, clean-up detail. Being on the clean-up crew may not be your idea of a good time, but it's a job that has to be done. Can you imagine what the world would be like if dead plants and animals remained on the surface of the earth? Combine this with the paper and beverage containers that we humans throw on the roadsides and you've got a real mess. Therefore, be thankful that clean-up is a way of life for some insects!

Termites are one of the insect cleaner-uppers. Their job is to help rid the world of dead trees. Termites destroy wood by eating it. However, eating wood is one thing, digesting it is another. To aid in wood digestion, termites have in their guts protozoa, which are microorganisms that break down cellulose.

All of this is a nice plan. However, when humans started building structures out of wood, the termites continued to do their ecological task. To a termite, dead wood is dead wood! It matters not that the wood is part of the finest house on the best street in town. Of course, when termites attack houses, people become hostile and call the little creatures pests and try and get rid of them.

Ogden Nash recognized the economic importance of termites as structural pests when he penned the following:

Some primal termites knocked on wood
And tasted it, and found it good,
And that is why your cousin May
Fell through the parlor floor today.

To many homeowners the thought of termites is a sober one indeed. In the springtime, at least in the case of termites, what has been out of sight comes to mind. It is in the spring that termites swarm. Swarming is a process where termites leave the underground nest chambers and disperse. This is one time in the year when the termites can be readily seen. But they can be easily confused with ants, which also swarm.

If termites are detected in a home, the best approach for control is to select a termite control service. However, do not panic! Termites work slowly, so you have time to purchase the service at your convenience. Also, choose a reliable firm; the termite business is one that is attractive to fly-by-night businesses.

Based on fossil records, termites are one of the oldest insects. So when termites eat the wood from which we have fashioned our houses, they are doing what comes naturally, as they have for the last 350 million years or so!

Some Insects Have a Lot of Nerve (Neuroptera)

The name of the insect order Neuroptera is derived from the Greek word neur, which means "nerve." Combined with pter, Greek for "wing," the order name literally means "nerve wing." It is a good name because the wings of Neuroptera are clear with numerous veins resembling a bunch of branched nerves.

Insects of the order Neuroptera are not among the most common insects. However, one group, the lacewings, are frequently found in our gardens. Lacewings are considered beneficial by gardeners because they are predators on aphids that are pests.

Some people think lacewings look like miniature prehistoric monsters. Scientists generally agree that insects are an ancient life form and, compared to humans, are prehistoric. However, the order Neuroptera is generally not considered to be among the oldest types of insects. They just look that way.

Lacewings are monsters when it comes to their eating habits. Like most species of Neuroptera, both adults and immatures feed on other animals, mostly insects. The adults have regular chewing mouthparts, and the immatures have sickle-like jaws that are used to suck the juices from prey. These larvae are sometimes called aphid lions in reference to their ferocious eating habits. Aphid lions have even been known to clamp down on a human now and then.

Lacewings have been called golden-eyed lacewing flies. Of course, they are not scientifically flies, even though they do fly. However, their eyes do have a metallic, golden color reflection in some lights. They also have been

called stink flies. This is based on the fact that they produce a disagreeable odor when handled.

Another group of Neuroptera are called ant lions. The ant lions get their name from the food of immatures, which is frequently ants. Immature ant lions dig pits to capture their food. The pits are located in sandy soil and are produced by the immature placing grains of sand on its head and then tossing the grains out of the pit. When completed, the pit is conical in shape with the ant lion residing in a hole at the base.

Unfortunate insects that tumble into the pit of an ant lion are consumed by the hungry occupant. Once the juices of the victim are consumed, the carcass is tossed from the pit like a rag doll.

There are several species of ant lions in the United States. They vary considerably in size, with some having a wing expanse of four inches. The adults have short, clubbed antennae and four similar wings. In general shape, they appear much like a damselfly. The eminent entomologist L. O. Howard wasn't impressed with their looks; in the *The Insect Book,* he wrote that the adult ant lions "are not especially attractive in their personal appearance."

Maybe the same should apply to other adult members of the Neuroptera. One group is called a snakefly, since it has an elongated prothorax and head with large eyes, much like a snake. There is also one called a mantipsid; it resembles a praying mantid with large grasping forelegs.

Probably the most fearsome looking of the Neuroptera are the dobsonflies, which are also called fishflies. With a wing spread of up to five inches, a fluttering flight and an attraction to light, this insect sometimes attracts a great deal of attention when it shows up near a porch light. This is especially true for the males, which have greatly enlarged mandibles protruding from the front of the head.

Immature dobsonflies are aquatic creatures called hellgrammites and are a favorite food of predatory fish like bass. Hellgrammites are also prized by fishermen as bait. But hellgrammites are not a docile-looking insect. Appropriate to the order name for this insect, it takes some nerve to put one on the hook!

A one-day old baby cockroach, about the size of a speck of dust, can run almost as fast as its parents.

The Doodlebug's Charm (Neuroptera)

James Whitcomb Riley, an Indiana poet, recognized a doodlebug when he saw one. In his poem "The Doodlebugs' Charm," Riley revealed that it was his Uncle Sidney who introduced him to the unusual six-legged creature. What was the fascination?

Doodlebugs are strange-looking insects with large, flat heads and long, protruding, sickle-like jaws. Like other members of the Neuroptera order, doodlebugs are predators on other insects.

Doodlebugs live in pits constructed of dry sand or dust. These pits can sometimes measure up to two inches wide at the soil surface. During construction the doodlebugs cleverly set traps by piling sand around the pits. Once inside their homes, the doodlebug eagerly waits for its meal to "drop in." One by one insects traveling too close to the pits tumble to the doodlebug's dinner tables. Ants are frequently their victims, giving rise to another common name for doodlebugs, "ant lions."

Doodlebugs are more common in the south and southwest of the United States. Their pits frequently are found in groups and in very dry conditions such as under buildings.

With a little strategy and a whole lot of patience, you may be able to entice a doodlebug to show itself. Instead of calling out its name, slowly push grains of sand into one of their pits. The curious and ravenous doodlebug will be tempted to investigate what it thinks is its next meal.

If you encounter a group of hungry larvae, then perhaps, like James Whitcomb Riley, you too, will discover the doodlebugs' charm.

Arsenic and Old Lacewings (Neuroptera)

Lacewings are the "arsenic and old lace" of the insect world. These insects are small—less than a half-inch in length. To us, they appear quite fragile, soft-bodied with four clear, membranous wings. The many cross-veins in their wings create an image, well, of lace—hence the name. But to their prey, lace-wings are as deadly as arsenic.

Lacewings, which are classified in the insect order Neuroptera, are considered ancient insects. Bearing resemblance to miniature prehistoric monsters, most are greenish or brown with golden-colored eyes. Their long antennae and fearsome chewing mouthparts suggest that lacewings are not part of the gentle, nectar-nipping set of the insect upper crust. Quite the opposite.

Both lacewing adults and larvae are random predators. They roam plants with the fervor of hungry diners scanning a menu as they search for insects. Aphids are a favorite food. Lacewing larvae have a pair of sickle-shaped jaws that are piercing-sucking tubes. When a prowling larva, appropriately called an aphid lion, encounters an aphid, the end is swift. The victim is impaled on the lacewing's sharp jaws and fluids are sucked from the victim's body like soda through a straw.

Larval lacewings are such dedicated predators that even their brothers and sisters are potential meals. Among lacewings, the first-hatched has an advantage. Newly hatched larvae begin a fervent search for food. Almost anything will do—even an unhatched lacewing egg. No amount of parental cajoling would likely prevent this ultimate expression of sibling rivalry. So lacewing mothers-to-be place their eggs on a stalk, just out of range of hungry little jaws. Of course, when larvae hatch and descend from the safe hatching perch, they're on their own in the dog-eat-dog world of lacewings and aphids.

Many gardeners have gained a great appreciation for the appetite of lacewings. In fact, lacewings have biological control potential and have even gained commercial status. Gardeners can purchase lacewings to help control the undesirable creatures that show up in their gardens—at least undesirable creatures of the insect variety. But lacewings are of no help whatsoever when it comes to hungry neighbors who seem to show up at the garden when the work is done and the harvest begins!

Insect Dragons (Odonata)

Skimmers, Biddies, and Darners. No, these aren't the latest rock bands. They are dragonflies.

Dragonflies are among the oldest insects. Some call them living fossils. Today's dragonflies look about like their ancestors that lived nearly 300 million years ago. Dragonflies roamed the skies during the 100-million-year reign of the dinosaurs. One such ancient dragonfly was itself dinosaur-sized. This insect had a wing span of nearly 27 inches.

Immature dragonflies, called nymphs, live in the water. Adults do fly far from water on their aerial forays, but they are most commonly found near water habitats.

Both adults and nymphs are predators. They feed primarily on other insects, although large dragonfly nymphs have been known to capture and devour small fish.

Adult dragonflies capture prey while on the wing. Although the dragonfly has a fearsome-looking set of jaws, it procures its meals by an unusual method. The dragonfly shapes its six legs into a basket. Then, in an insect version of an aerial dogfight, overtakes prey from behind, snaring the potential meal in its legs.

The dragonfly sometimes eats on the wing—sort of a "meal to go" in the insect world. For a more leisurely dining experience, the dragonfly will perch on vegetation before devouring the hapless victim.

Because dragonflies destroy a number of insects, including mos-

quitoes, gnats and flies, they are beneficial. Even though dragonflies are predators, they are harmless to people. These insects neither sting nor bite. However, dragonflies have not always been considered harmless.

There are a number of superstitions associated with the dragonflies. For instance, in some rural areas of the United States, the common name "snake doctor" was acquired because people assumed that the dragonfly acted as a guard to snakes. This may have originated because both snakes and dragonflies share marshy habitats.

Another superstition held that dragonflies could sew together various parts of the human body, including lips, nostrils, eyelids and ears. This belief gave rise to the common name darning needle or devil's darning needle.

Some of the fear of dragonflies, and some of the superstitions, are probably based on the fearsome look of the insect. However, part of the mystique of the dragonfly is due to its territorial nature. Male dragonflies set up territories, just as do certain birds and mammals. The dragonfly then defends its territory against other dragonflies. Such territorial defense leads to spectacular battles among these master aerialists. The dragonflies also check out other intruders in their territory—a surveillance activity that some folks might interpret as hostile behavior.

The next time you spy a beautiful, brightly colored dragonfly doing aerial maneuvers, pause for a moment and watch closely. You are watching an animal that has been flying for 300 million years. With all of that practice it's no wonder dragonflies are good at flying!

Hoppers, Hoppers Everywhere (Orthoptera)

Very few groups of insects have caused more problems for humankind than grasshoppers. The destructive nature of these insects has been vividly described in the Bible. The Old Testament chronicles several instances of damage by grasshoppers, including Joel 2:3, "...the land is as the Garden of Eden before them and behind them a desolate wilderness; yea, and nothing shall escape them."

So common was grasshopper damage in ancient times that the Hebrew Bible includes at least nine words for these insects. The words might have represented different stages, or even different species, but clearly describe the insects we know as grasshoppers.

The eighth of the ten plagues visited upon Egypt preceding the Exodus was a great mass of locusts. "Locust" is the term used worldwide for the migratory grasshoppers common in northern Africa.

As a general rule, grasshopper populations and levels of destruction are higher in regions with limited rainfall—thus the high incidence in parts of Africa. Also, there are more grasshopper problems in the drier western states of the United States than in the east.

Years that lack rainfall sometimes are remembered by farmers as "grasshopper years." Such was the case in the 1930s. During this decade, most areas of the United States experienced high grasshopper populations and destruction. The extreme number of hoppers totally destroyed the farmers' crops, so the pests had to look for dinner elsewhere. Stories of these

insects eating the handles out of pitchforks and severely damaging straw hats left outside are common.

While the word "grass" is in their name, grasshoppers will readily feed on most kinds of plants. For that reason, these insects can be pests to farmers and gardeners alike. Grasshopper damage is normally not evident until the middle part of the growing season. For instance, corn almost never shows damage until it is at least waist high.

The onset of grasshopper damage is related to how grasshoppers overwinter. Most grasshoppers spend the winter in the egg stage. A female grasshopper uses her abdomen to deposit an egg mass in the soil. Each egg mass contains from 20 to 120 eggs. These eggs hatch in late spring and early summer. The newly hatched nymphs are very small, have small appetites, and largely are unnoticed by most people.

As the grasshopper nymphs grow, they will go through four to five molts before adulthood. Increased size means an increased appetite. Consequently, in a month to six weeks after hatching, the young hoppers are chewing up a lot of plant tissue. Once they become adults they continue to eat, so by August in much of the United States, grasshoppers are doing maximum damage to plants.

The adults mate and the females begin to lay eggs in August and September. Each female will deposit up to 25 egg masses, destined to become next year's hoppers.

So if this is a hopper year for you, be thankful that not all of the 600 or so grasshopper species in the United States are in your backyard. Or you can do as folks, including John the Baptist, did in biblical times and eat the hoppers. I hear dry roasted they taste a little bit like chicken.

Katydids Do It in the Trees (Orthoptera)

One of the sounds commonly heard during the nighttime hours during August and September in eastern hardwood forests is that of the katydid. So exuberant are these insect songsters that their efforts sometimes produce a crescendo of deafening proportions—a swell of sound so overwhelming that it can be described as the noise of the forest night.

These tree-dwelling insects appear to engage in shouting matches. "Proclaim it from the highest tree tops" is the operating philosophy of the "singing" katydid. The sound produced might not be much of a song, but it is the basis for the name katydid. The song is either two or three syllables and, to some early listeners anyway, it sounded as if the insect was crying "Katy Did, Katy Did, Katy Did." Listen closely to katydids singing, and you can notice that some seem to say "Katy Didn't."

Because of the two songs, a group of singing katydids seem to be in a shouting match about whether Katy did or Katy didn't. What it is that Katy did or didn't do is not apparent from this vociferous exchange.

It is the male of the species that sings in most insects, and that is the case with the katydid. The song is used by the male to attract the female of the species. The sounds that are a bit noisy to us are apparently sweet-sounding to the female katydid, because she follows the tones to a rendezvous with the crooner.

The sex of the insect doing the singing has not always been clear to those listening to the katydid song. For instance, the poet Philip Freneau wrote these lines about the insect and its song:

In her suit of green arrayed,
Hear her singing in the shade
Caty-did, Caty-did, Caty-did!

Freneau got the color correct. The green is a functional hue so the insect can blend into the tree leaves where they live, but he mistakenly attributed the song to the female—hear her singing! He also used the letter c rather than k to describe the sound.

Regardless of how you spell it, the sound of katydids is common where trees abound. It is a sound not always appreciated by everyone. Some years ago, a friend of mine from a large city complained that he had trouble sleeping at our house in the late summer because of the noise—noise dominated by singing katydids in the woods nearby. To each his own, I suppose. I would much rather listen to noisy katydids than the blare of sirens and car horns that seem to dominate the nighttime sounds in metropolitan areas.

Cricket Sounds Attract Attention (Orthoptera)

Crickets are among the most recognizable of insect singers. Since crickets are distributed worldwide, few people have not heard these insects sing.

To be sure, the response to the song varies. A homeowner might assume the song portends damage to clothing or curtains—a reasonable concern, since crickets generally feed on dead plant material and will chew holes in cotton fabric.

Generally though, the song of the cricket is admired by humanity. In some parts of the world, especially in the Orient, crickets are confined to cages so that people can enjoy the song. These cages can be ornately designed. When fastened to a belt or carried in a pocket, cricket cages, with their resident musicians, become a miniature "boombox" for their owners.

It is the male cricket that sings. The sound is produced to attract females and to warn other males. Even though we humans might describe it as grinding gears, it must sound sweet to the females, who happily mate and produce the next generation of crickets.

Most crickets, and other singing insects as well, are soloists. While it may appear that groups of crickets are chirping in unison, it is probably an accident. Singing crickets might, however, prompt other insects to join the activity.

The rate of chirping in crickets is related to the temperature. When the temperature is high, the chirp is faster and therefore higher-pitched than sounds produced at lower temperatures. The entomologist A. E. Dolbear

worked out a formula for determining the temperature based on the number of insect sounds per minute. For instance for the house cricket the formula is:

$$\text{Temperature} = (50 + ((\text{No. Chirps/ Min}) - 40)) \div 4$$

Sound produced by the snowy tree cricket has some interesting aspects to it. These insects are small white crickets that are found on tree leaves and branches in late fall. Their sound is a soft, high-pitched trill. While the stridulating crickets fill the woods with their crooning it is difficult to trace the sound to a particular cricket. It is almost as if these rather ghostly-looking insects are insect ventriloquists.

Even more surprising is the fact that female snowy tree crickets lack auditory organs with which to hear the sound. So why do male snowy tree crickets fill the woods with sound each fall? Well, it might be for territory. An insect shout that says, "This limb is mine!" When the males sing, the raised wings expose a gland on the upper surface of the body that produces an odor that attracts the female. So maybe the male is just singing in joyous anticipation of the arrival of a potential mate!

Insect Biology

Insects are segmented, mindless creatures that breathe through holes in their sides. They are covered with an exoskeleton that must be shed to accommodate growth. Insects walk on six jointed legs, and some fly with four wings, while others use two wings to stay airborne. Some immature insects don't have legs at all; they just wiggle from place to place. Insects look at the world through eyes with many lens, some smell with their antennae, and others taste with their feet. Insects don't have ears on their heads, but these sound detection devices are found on their legs, their abdomen, or their thorax. Insect ears pick up sounds of all kinds, including the clicks and scrapes produced when insects rub body parts together.

Young insects may look totally different from their parents and if so likely don't feed on the same type food. Adults of most species of insects survive for only a matter of weeks. There are, however, several insect species whose adults live for many years, and a few species where the adult life is a single day. Some species vomit on their food. Others attract mates with perfume or lights. Some even make a meal of their mate. Many can be frozen solid and survive, while others fly 3,000 miles to avoid winter.

Insects and humans are not very much alike, even though both are members of the animal kingdom. In fact, these two dominant types of animals on the earth are exact opposites in many ways, including physical structure. It has been said that insects, compared to humans, are inside out and upside down. Insects are inside out, because their skeleton is on the outside, ours the inside. The relative position of the central nerve cord and the heart are reversed in insects compared to humans. Our nerve cord is in

the vertebrae that form the backbone, in insects it is the tube-like heart that occupies that position—without the backbone, of course. So we say these six-legged creatures are upside down in comparison to the human animal.

No matter how you look at it, insects and humans are very different animals. But both creatures are very successful.

The symbol of the scarab bettle (a dung beetle) was sacred to the ancient Egyptians, who associated them with the god of the rising sun. They carved names, designs, and symbols onto the abdomen of the dead insects and wore them as jewelry. They even attached them over the hearts of mummies, with the belief that they would help the deceased as they stood judgment in the afterlife.

Insects Are Schizophrenic

Psychologists would no doubt classify many insects as schizophrenic. After all, during their lives, several species of insects clearly possess a split personality. But unlike human schizophrenics, these insects not only have a change in personality, they also look different! That is because of a biological process known as metamorphosis. Through metamorphosis, the insects change between forms that are distinctly different in the way they look, in the types of food they eat, and in the way they behave.

The forms are so completely different that we have different names for each. Maggots, caterpillars, and grubs are terms used for immatures of some insects. The corresponding adults are called flies, butterflies, and beetles.

For insects, changing personalities is not a quick change; it is a major undertaking. To do so the insect employs a variation of the old superman trick of running into a telephone booth. The change of the immature to the adult occurs in a stage during which it's known as the pupa.

In the pupal stage, the insect undergoes a remarkable remaking that surpasses the best work of the most skilled plastic surgeons. But the insect starts at the ground floor. It doesn't simply readjust what is already there, it starts over. Old tissues from the immature are broken down and reassembled into the new adult.

In general, the pupal stage of insects is immobile. A pupa can wiggle around a little, but it is incapable of moving from place to place. Thus the insect pupa cannot run away from predators or move to get out of the sun or rain. So the immature insect has to seek a place for pupation. A caterpillar may crawl several meters looking for just the right spot to pupate. When it finds a suitable location, it will form a cell in the soil, fold leaves around itself, or spin a cocoon.

Some of the most conspicuous pupae belong to the butterflies and moths. Generally, moths cover their pupae with cocoons, although some do not. Cocoons are spun of silk, and it is from the cocoon of the silkworm that we produce the silken thread that is used to make silk cloth. The pupae of butterflies are known as naked pupae, since they do not spin cocoons. As a rule, these naked pupae are attached to twigs or leaves.

Pupae of butterflies and moths are known by the name chrysalis, which is based on the Greek root "chrys," meaning "gold." (We find the same root in "chrysanthemum," which literally means "gold flower.") The basis for the name was that some butterfly chrysalids, such as that of the monarch, have prominent gold flecks.

What a story! An ugly plant-devouring, crawling worm disappears behind a gold-flecked cape and emerges as a beautiful, winged butterfly.

Have Wings, Will Fly

Birds do it. But so do the bees. In fact, most insects are real experts at it. They've been cruising the airways of planet Earth for 350 million years or so.

Insects have so mastered the art of flight that it is one of the reasons for their success. Indeed, in honor of their winged proficiency, we call some of them "flies."

As landlubbers, we humans stand in awe of the aerial gymnastics performed by insects. Scientists have studied insect flight and even counted the number of beats of an insect wing. A swallowtail butterfly, for instance, will flap its wings about nine times a second. A honey bee has a wingbeat frequency of 250 beats per second; the old house fly, about 190; and some mosquitoes, a little over 300. It is the frequency of the wingbeat that produces the mosquito's all-too-familiar humming sound.

House flies cruise along at nearly 5 miles per hour. Some sphinx moths are the fastest insect fliers, reaching a top speed of over 33 miles per hour. The honey bee can fly about 8 miles per hour, and the bumblebee can buzz along at 11 miles per hour, a respectable speed considering that a scientist once calculated that a bumble bee couldn't fly at all.

It seems that the surface area of the bumble bee wing was too small to carry that fuzzy, yellow-and-black-striped body aloft. Of course, folks who have been dive-bombed by a bee intent on causing bodily harm have experienced the error of that calculation firsthand!

Insects use the power of flight for many purposes, including finding

mates, avoiding enemies, and moving to a new territory. Some insects travel many miles on the wing. The champion traveler in this regard is the monarch butterfly. This insect travels each year from its breeding grounds in Canada to overwintering sites in the mountains of Mexico—a trip of over 2,000 miles.

Of the teeming billions of insects, not all use flight as a preferred form of locomotion. Some prefer to hoof it, as this old poem tells:

> The June bug hath a gaudy wing,
> The lighting bug a flame,
> The bedbug hath no wing at all,
> But he gets there just the same!

Antennae Aren't Just for Space Aliens

Some people respond to insects as if they were creatures from another world. Maybe it's because they look otherworldly. The jointed legs, exoskeleton, multifaceted eyes, and the antennae do give insects a far-out appearance.

To be sure, the human animal has eyes, legs, and a skeleton, although somewhat different from those of insects. But when it comes to antennae, we humans have been shut out, dealt a big zero by Mother Nature.

We generally have less than an outpouring of enthusiasm for nature's creatures with antennae. That includes the insects. Maybe it's because insects wave their antennae in our faces from time to time. Or maybe it's because we're jealous that we don't have similar structures.

Actually, we should be jealous. Antennae are marvelous structures that allow insects to gather information about their environment. Hairs on the antennae of some insects pick up vibrations in the air and allow the insect to hear. This is the way some male midges and mosquitoes detect their mates. The sound of the vibrating wings of the female are detected by the antennae of the male.

Both taste and smell are associated with antennae in some insects. The chemical clues detected include alarm chemicals produced by other insects of the same species. That is the reason ants very quickly come to the aid of a nest mate that has been injured or killed. Chemicals produced by female moths sometimes can be detected five miles downwind by a male of the same species—all because the chemical is picked up by his antennae.

In addition, insects are able to identify suitable plants on which to lay their eggs because of the odor of the plant. Many times, the plant odor is detected by sensors on the antennae. It is also the way flies find dead animals.

Some parasitic wasps actually use their antennae as a dog uses its nose, to trail another species. These wasps will tap their antennae on a surface as they attempt to follow a specific insect. When they find it, their goal is a sinister one. They will try to lay an egg on or in the creature, an egg that will hatch into a larva, which will feed on the parasitized insect.

There are many kinds of insect antennae, and all of them have names. For instance, many grasshoppers, crickets, and cockroaches have long antennae with segments that are about the same size from base to tip. These threadlike structures are called filiform and are great for waving around.

Some antennae, such as those of butterflies, have a knob on the end and are called capitate. The antennae of moths don't have a knob on the end. Instead, they generally are fuzzy, a condition termed plumose.

Some insects seem to have a flag at the end of their antennae, which are then said to be lamellate. Some are bent in the middle and are called geniculate. Such is the case with ant antennae. That is good to know because that is one way to tell an ant from a termite. The antennae of termites aren't geniculate; they are more threadlike.

Whatever they are called, those insect antennae are busy picking up signals—hopefully not from outer space!

A Tale of Blood and Guts of the Insect Type

Some time back, I received a letter with a request to identify insects that a homeowner had discovered in his house. Were they ants? Termites? Or something even worse? The insects were enclosed in a small plastic bag. The envelope—and its contents—had been processed through an automated stamp-canceling machine. and in this case, more than the stamp was cancelled. The insects were smashed to smithereens.

Now smashing insects is not something new to humans. We smack insects every chance that we get. Fly swatters were invented for just that purpose. But we will use our hands, newspapers, and even our hats as insect-whacking devices when necessary.

Whenever we are successful in smacking an insect, what remains doesn't bear much resemblance to the intact creature. To be sure, you can sometimes find an identifiable wing, a leg or two, and maybe even an antenna, but the most obvious remnant is a greasy, gooey little spot. We're talking insect blood and guts here.

Most people have some notion about how the outside of an insect looks. You know, it has three major body sections. There is a head in the front with a mouth, eyes and antennae. A middle section, with wings and legs attached, called the thorax is next. Then comes the abdomen, which literally brings up the rear. But most people don't think much about insect guts. At least, not until they look at their hand after terminating a fly or when they struggle to clean the car windshield after a warm summer night's drive.

The blood and guts of insects are every bit as important to them as our innards are to us. However, there are some differences. Both insects and humans have important fluids that flow through the body. We call ours blood. In insects, that fluid is called hemolymph.

Human blood flows through a series of tubes. On the way to the heart, those tubes are veins; away from the heart and lungs, the tubes are arteries. Insects don't have a series of tubes to transmit such fluid. The insect hemolymph just sloshes around in a bag—a bag that we call the insect body. Scientifically, the human system is closed. Insects, on the other hand, have an open system.

Closed and open is not the only difference in the internal fluid systems of insects and humans. In mammals, including humans, blood carries oxygen to the cells and carbon dioxide away. The exchange occurs in the lungs. It is a red substance called hemoglobin that is the carrier, which is why our blood is red.

Insect blood does not carry oxygen. It lacks hemoglobin and is not red, except in a very few insects. (For example, aquatic larvae of a group of flies called chironomids are known as bloodworms because they have hemoglobin in their blood; this is also true of the larva of a bot fly and a bug called a backswimmer.) The hemolymph of most insects is either colorless or yellow.

Another major component of insect innards is the digestive tract. It would normally contain food in various states of digestion. The inside of an insect would also include what is known as fat body. Insects, like humans, store energy in the form of fat. In insects, the fat is stored in specialized cells that are located throughout the inside of the insect.

So the next time you see a smashed insect don't just think greasy,

grimy insect guts. Be scientific and think hemolymph, undigested gut contents, and fat body cells! And look closely, because there ought to be some wings and legs thrown in there somewhere.

The earliest fossil cockroach is about 280 million years old—80 million years older than the first dinosaurs.

In Insects, the Eyes Have It!

Nothing is more important to adult insects than their eyes. Looking casually at insects, most humans are more likely to notice other appendages first— legs, wings, and antennae, for instance. But to the insect, the eyes are just as important as these more obvious protrusions.

To be sure, legs allow insects to run, jump, and cling. Their wings provide the power of flight. Antennae are wonderful devices for smelling. But the eyes play very important roles in many aspects of insect lives.

Some insects, those like lice and fleas that are parasitic, don't have eyes at all. A few insects have single-lens eyes, but most adult insects have compound eyes. In some insects, the number of lenses is in the thousands. In dragonflies, the number of lenses is more than 10,000.

Because of compound eyes, entomologists assume that insects don't "see" in the same way that humans do. A single lens in an eye allows a sharply defined image. The multiple lenses in compound eyes probably, at best, produce a blurred image.

But then, the goal of the insect eye is not to provide the clearest image but to keep in visual contact with a large area. That is the reason that eyes sometimes occupy a sizable portion of the insect head. The eyes also frequently bulge out to develop a wide field of vision.

In some insects, such as dragonflies and some flies, the eyes actually meet in the midline of the head. Through multiple lenses, these insect eyes function much as a radar system that continually rotates, scanning the horizon. And the purpose is much the same: to pick up anything within sight.

While insect eyes might not provide the clearest image, they do provide an excellent motion detector. That is the reason it is difficult to sneak up on an insect. Insects need such protection, since it seems the world is out to get them—primarily to make a meal out of them. This is the case in insect eaters, such as birds and frogs.

Humans sometimes just want to remove the insect from the face of the earth. We developed such things as fly swatters to aid us in the task. But you still have to be quick, since it is a sure bet that the fly sees the swatter coming and many times manages to escape.

Insects also use their eyes to judge distance. This is important to predaceous insects that need to catch other insects for their food. The praying mantid uses its eyes for that purpose. By looking at a potential insect meal, it is able to accurately assess the distance to the prey, based on the view from several different lenses. It therefore waits until the prey is within range before grabbing for it.

Insect eyes are also sensitive to UV light waves. Such sensitivity allows the insect to see things that we humans cannot. Honey bees detect the UV patterns on flowers. Night-flying insects navigate using UV light. That is the reason that UV traps are so effective in luring insects to their deaths in an electric grid.

Polarized light is also detected by insects. Honey bees navigate based on the polarized light from the sky. This is known as the light-compass reaction where the insect can detect the pattern of polarized light from a patch of blue sky.

So to an insect, "I can see clearly now" doesn't have much meaning. Insect eyes are more UV light and movement sensors. But the system seems to work, since insects don't have trouble finding their way or avoiding predators.

The Madagascar hissing cockroach is one of the few insects that give birth to live young, rather than laying eggs.

Stripteasing—Insect Style

Insects and their arthropod relatives, such as shrimp, crabs, and lobsters, possess exoskeletons, a combination skin-and-skeleton that protects them against crushing, scratching, invasion by microorganisms, and water loss. A hard, durable exoskeleton is a great protective device, but it is a real problem as the insect grows—it doesn't stretch.

Knights of old who protected themselves with suits of armor had a similar problem at times. Indeed, the knight who forgot to mind his waistline discovered the need for a new suit. Insects face a similar problem several times during their life cycles, and like the ancient knights, they acquire new suits of armor.

Before an insect grows a new exoskeleton, it sheds the old one, a process called molting. Most people are familiar with the shed skins of insects. What youngster hasn't gathered the conspicuous shells of cicadas? When the immature cicada nymph emerges from its underground home, it immediately molts to the winged adult stage. The old exoskeleton can be found fastened to a tree, shrub, or fence post. Aphids also molt, and sometimes the only evidence of these pest insects on a plant will be hundreds of white ghost-like skins.

Insect molting has long fascinated scientists, who have worked hard to describe the chemical nature of the process. Even poets have noticed and described the magic of an insect shedding its skin. In Tennyson's "The Two Voices," we read about a dragonfly molting:

An inner impulse rent the veil
Of his old husk; from head to tail
Came out clear plates of sapphire mail.

The ancient Greeks were aware of the molting process and had a word to describe it: *ecdysis* (eck DEE sis). It was from this word that H. L. Mencken coined his humorous term for a stripteaser—an ecdysiast.

The practical nature of an insect molting might not hold the same attraction to most people as the dance of a stripteaser. However, the result is the same; both the insect and the ecdysiast end up removing their outer clothing.

Insect Legs Are Not Just for Walking

One of the defining characteristics of adult insects is that they have six legs. In some historical scientific circles, insects actually were called hexapods, based on leg number.

With the immature insects, however, it's another matter. Some immatures, like fly maggots, don't have any legs. Others, like caterpillars, have more than three pairs of legs. (Technically, those caterpillars still have six legs; the things that look like legs are called prolegs, but they function in a similar fashion to legs.)

Insect legs come in many sizes and shapes. You can learn a lot about an insect by looking at the way the legs are shaped. For instance, many insect legs are very much like human legs in structure. Both insects and humans have a leg part called a femur. We call it our thigh bone. Below that, in both insect and human legs, is a tibia. We call that our shin bone. The bones making up our feet are called tarsae. The same is true of insects. Our legs and the similar insect legs function to run or walk. Insects like cockroaches, ladybugs, and fireflies have legs that function to walk or run.

Legs in insects exhibit many modifications from the basic walking shape. For instance, the front legs of camel crickets look like miniature shovels. The insect uses the front legs to dig its burrow. Dung beetles have front legs that are similar to those of the cave cricket. The dung beetles use forelegs to dig, but also to fashion balls of mammal dung. The dung, or manure, is buried in the ground and is the food for immature dung beetles.

Some insects, such as crickets, grasshoppers, katydids, and fleas, have hind legs modified for jumping. All of these insects are well-known for their ability to jump when attempting to escape from danger.

The front legs on some insects are designed for grasping. The praying mantid has legs like that. Mantids use their forelegs to catch and hold the insects that become their food. The same is true of other insects that make meals of their cousins. Water striders use their front legs for grasping, as do the predators known as assassin bugs.

Dragonflies and damselflies have legs that function mainly for perching on plants. But these insects use their legs to form a basket, which is used to trap small flying insects when the dragonfly overtakes them in flight.

Insects that live in water have legs shaped like paddles for swimming. Lice have legs that are designed to grasp the hair of their hosts. In fact, many insect legs have devices that allow them to cling to things: claws for hooking into something soft and sticky pads for hard, slick surfaces like glass. Many insects have both claws and sticky pads, so they are equipped to walk on or hang on almost any surface.

Insects also use their legs for functions other than locomotion and grasping. Several grasshoppers, crickets, and katydids have legs with combs that are used with other legs or wings to produce sound.

Some butterflies and flies have taste buds in their feet. This allows them to taste any item on which they are standing. For butterflies, they use the information to find a host plant for egg-laying. For flies, the information tells them if the item they are standing on is good to eat. If so, they extend their mouthparts and begin to feed.

Other modifications of insect legs are to help camouflage the insect. Some insects that feed on plants have legs that resemble leaves to help them blend into their environment.

Another unusual modification of an insect's legs is found in the honey bee. Honey bees have a pollen basket on their back legs. They collect the pollen from their hair with a comb on a leg and place it in the basket for transport to the hive. So honey bees observed with yellow blobs on their legs are pollen collectors with their pollen baskets filled.

It is apparent that insects use their legs for many different functions other than just locomotion. They have to; after all, they don't have a pair of legs modified into arms as we humans do.

Insect Mouths Have a Story to Tell

An old adage holds that we are what we eat. And as my mother often reminded me in my younger days, how we eat also speaks volumes.

Insects don't have mothers who harp on the importance of table manners, but how insects eat does tell a story. The structure of insect mouths is
related to their food and how they consume it.

An insect's mouth varies in structure from species to species and is one
of the characteristics that scientists use to classify insects into groups. Most
insect mouths can be categorized as one of six major types.

First, there is the chewing type. This is the type of mouth that scientists believe was the most primitive of insect mouths. Chewing insects have
mandibles that cut off and grind the food—just as humans have mandibles
for the same purpose. Many common insects possess chewing-type mouths,
including grasshoppers and crickets, cockroaches, praying mantises, beetles,
dragonflies, and most wasps. Caterpillars, the immature forms of butterflies
and moths, also have chewing mouth parts.

Many of the insects with chewing mouths, such as grasshoppers,
beetles, and caterpillars, feed on living plants. Crickets, cockroaches, and some
beetles have to chew up dead stuff for food. Praying mantids, dragonflies, many
wasps, and some beetles are predators and must chew up their insect prey.

Other insects, like the non-biting flies, have a sponging-type mouth.
Like the house fly, these insects can eat only liquid food. Sometimes, if the
item is a solid, the insect will vomit saliva on the potential food to turn it into
a liquid. The liquid can then be sponged up.

Some biting flies, like horse and deer flies, have a cutting, sponging type of mouth. These insects cut the host's skin to cause blood to flow. The blood is then sponged up with the mouth parts, much the same way a surgical team would sponge up blood during an operation.

Many insects consume juices as food. These insects frequently have what are called piercing-sucking mouths. They have a hollow needle that is used to pierce plants in order to drink sap. Aphids, leafhoppers, and cicadas feed in this way. Some insects use the same technique to drink blood from their prey. Mosquitoes, lice, fleas, and bed bugs sup in this way.

Other insects also feed on liquids, but only if the liquids are free for the taking. Butterflies and moths have a siphoning tube for this function. The tube is called a proboscis and is generally curled up under the head of the insect when not in use. When the butterfly wants a sip of nectar, it uncoils the tube to produce a straw for sipping nectar from the flower. They also drink water in the same way.

Honey bees and bumble bees have a combination of chewing and drinking mouths. Called chewing-lapping mouths, they can drink nectar and chew holes in most materials. That is how they sip nectar from a flower and chew up the wax to form the comb in the hive.

So like humans, how an insect eats sends a message. The chewers, like the caterpillars, chomp and rip their food with little thought to manners. On the other hand, butterflies sip their food in such a prim and proper way that even Miss Manners would be proud. Who would know that based on their eating habits the caterpillar could ever turn into a refined butterfly? Human moms take heart! There is hope for that chomping and chewing teenage son in the house.

Insects Bite and Sting for Good Reasons

Most people understand that some insects bite and some insects sting—just two of the reasons that many folks don't like insects. In fact, biting and stinging might be the main reasons that humans hate insects in general.

Insects haven't taken to biting and stinging humans just to be mean. Biting and stinging behavior is associated with survival of these six-legged creatures. Such activity is generally related to food for the insect or its offspring. Take, for instance, the bite of a mosquito. It has to do with getting a blood meal. The same is true for horse flies, deer flies, and stable flies when they bite.

Stinging can be related to procuring a meal for the offspring. Many wasps use a stinger to paralyze an insect as food for their babies. That is why a cicada killer wasp stings a cicada and drags it to a hole in the ground for the offspring.

In other instances, the sting functions to defend the insect or its colony from harm. Wasps will sting for that reason, although they also use their stingers to procure food. Bees, on the other hand, only use their stingers as defensive weapons.

Insect stings cause pain and suffering to recipient animals. And that is the way the insect wants it to be. The sting is designed to get the animal to let go of the insect or run away from the nest.

So which insect has the worst sting? It probably depends on whom you ask. There really hasn't been much research on the subject. A few years ago, Christopher Starr wrote an article entitled "A Pain Scale for Bee, Wasp and Ant Stings." Starr concludes that the severity of stinging is related to "the number of potential defenders of the colony, their readiness to attack, and the effectiveness of a single sting."

The first two stinging severity categories, numbers and willingness to attack, are easy to understand. Especially by any of us who at some time in our misspent youth intentionally disturbed a bumble bee or hornet nest in order to incite a human and insect war. This, I have been told, is primarily an activity of young boys! Rest assured, though, that the human participants quickly learn that insect numbers and willingness to attack have a direct relationship to pain from insect stings.

The third category, the one dealing with the effectiveness of a single sting, is difficult to define. The reason is that the severity of an insect sting is related to the type of poison, the amount of poison, the structure of the stinger, and the reaction of the animal to the sting. For instance, some people are allergic to the poison used by insects in stings. In this case, the person will show such a severe reaction to the poison that they could die without medical treatment.

For most people, though, the response to an insect sting is local pain and swelling. As a true scientist, Starr ranked insect stings on a pain scale of 1 to 4 where 1 is slight pain and 4 traumatically painful. On this scale, the sting of a honey bee, bumble bee, or yellow jacket is rated a 2. A paper wasp, like those that build nests under the eves, was given a 3—sharply and seriously painful. South American bullet ants were ranked 4.

However, we know that the pain of a sting varies among people. Sometimes the pain gets less as an individual gets stung more often. Bee keepers can become tolerant to honey bee stings during the summer season. On the other hand, some people become more susceptible as they get more stings and, at some point, might exhibit such a severe reaction that medical treatment becomes necessary.

Insect bites also vary from person to person in the amount of pain they inflict. For instance, when a mosquito bites, there may be little or no pain experienced by the victim. That is the way the insect wants it to be, since it would like to take a blood meal without the donor noticing. However, the chemical it injects to keep the blood from clotting causes the irritation we know as mosquito bites and the amount of irritation varies from person to person.

So the severity of insect bites and stings depends on the insect and on the reaction of the person. But rest assured that insects have a reason for bites and stings—and it's not just to make us suffer!

Insects Don't Add; They Multiply

Ever wonder how there can be so many insects in so quickly after the spring thaw? It could be magic, or spontaneous generation. But it isn't either.

It has to do with the birds and the bees—mainly the bees! Bees and other insects are very good at laying eggs in very large numbers. Scientists believe that rapid reproduction is one reason for the phenomenal success of insects on earth.

Consider the honey bee queen. In the warm months of June and July, she can lay between 1,500 and 2,000 eggs each day. Since she must deposit each in a cell of the comb, that production represents a good day's work. You might say she's "busy as a bee" during that time. A honey bee queen will produce around 100,000 eggs during her average three-year life span. Not a bad record.

But honey bee egg production pales in comparison to that of the large queen termites of Africa. Such queens, real egg-laying machines, may lay as many as 36,000 eggs in 24 hours. That's about 25 eggs a minute and totals over 13,000,000 per year. Such queen termites are believed to live between 50 and 100 years. That figures out to be over a billion eggs produced by one queen.

While the old house fly is no queen termite when it comes to laying eggs, she isn't a slouch either. Average egg production during the life of a house fly is probably around 800 eggs. The record number of eggs measured for one fly is 2,387. But the success of the house fly is not solely due to the

rate of egg-laying; it is also due to the speed with which the insect goes through its life cycle.

The same is true for the fruit fly, an insect that almost everyone recognizes. Fruit flies seem to magically appear around overripe vegetables or fruit. The appearance of large numbers of fruit flies in a short time shows how fast this insect develops. Under ideal conditions, fruit flies may produce 25 generations per year. Each female may lay up to 100 eggs, of which about half will hatch into females and half into males.

It has been calculated that by starting with one pair of fruit flies and allowing the original and all succeeding females to reproduce under ideal conditions for one year, the number of flies would be fantastic—about 10^{41}. (That's 10 with 41 zeros behind it.) All those flies would form a ball 96 million miles in diameter, if you assume that 1,000 would fit in a cubic inch. A ball that size would almost reach the sun from the earth!

Of course, all insects that hatch don't survive to reproduce. Many insects die of starvation or exposure to lethal temperatures or are consumed as food by other animals. Among insects, many are hatched so that a few survive. You could say that in the insect world, the battle cry is, "The more, the merrier!"

Insect Songsters

Insects rival birds as the animal world's most noteworthy singers. The rasps, shrills, clicks, and chirps of insects aren't as melodious as the tones produced by birds, but by sheer volume the insects frequently dominate their avian competition in nature's chorus.

Unlike birds, insects use a variety of mechanisms to harmonize. Some, like mosquitoes and bees, produce sound by the vibration of their wings.

Such sound is incidental to the activity of these insects. However, the mosquito's whine has come to be a warning to its human victims. Likewise, the buzzing of bees is widely recognized as a danger sign in the animal world. Some flies even mimic the sound for their own protection. And the sound is so familiar that the composer Rimski-Korsakov used violins to represent it in his popular "Flight of the Bumblebee."

The majority of insect choristers produce sound by stridulation. That is, they rub one body part against another. Some grasshoppers produce sound by rubbing the edges of their wings together. Others "fiddle" by rubbing the back leg across the edge of the wing.

But not all insects are fiddlers. Some are drummers. The cicadas are the percussionists of the insect world. The drum of the cicada is a membrane located on the abdomen, which is vibrated by the use of a complicated set of muscles to produce the well-known hum of the cicada.

Insect sounds vary throughout the season and over the course of the day. For example, many grasshoppers sing during the day but become silent at nightfall. Many crickets begin to warble when the sun goes down.

Insects sing primarily to communicate with others of their species. For instance, some insects court a potential mate by crooning a sweet song, a practice the insects share with birds and, in some instances, humans.

Unlike humans, the male of the species is usually the lead singer. This fact was noted long ago by the Greek philosopher Xenarchus, who wrote, "Happy are the cicadas lives for they have voiceless wives."

Many people over the years have enjoyed the harmonic renditions of insects. Some Oriental cultures keep crickets in cages just for the beauty of their singing. Indeed, a cricket chirping in the house is considered good luck. Such an idea was noted by Charles Dickens in his story "The Cricket on the Hearth."

However, not all people regard the sound of insects as a thing of joy. For instance, an innovative entomology student once proclaimed on a test that cicada killers kill cicadas because "They can't stand the noise!"

"Nosy" Insects Mind Own Business

What do elephants, Jimmy Durante, and some insects have in common? They all have a proboscis.

Technically, a proboscis is any tubular process on the head of an animal. The trunk of the elephant and the protruding mouths of some insects certainly fit the criteria. We also use the term "proboscis" as a humorous term for the human nose. That is especially true when the nose is a bit larger than normal.

The proboscises of insects can generally be grouped into three types. There is the piercing-sucking type of proboscis. This design enables the insect to extract liquids from within a living organism. Some plant bugs pierce plant tissue and imbibe sap from the plant. Aphids also are sap suckers and, in the process, sometimes damage plants by taking a bit more sap than the plant can stand to lose.

Mammals, including humans, also are susceptible to losing fluids such as blood due to feeding of some insects bearing proboscises. Some lice are called sucking lice because they use their proboscises to suck blood from the host. Female mosquitoes have a proboscis that is used to procure a blood meal from some unlucky animal.

Some flies, such as the house fly, have a proboscis that is equipped with a sponge-like device on the bottom. Such insects are considered to have sponging-siphoning mouthparts.

Weevils are insects that have their chewing-type mouths extended from their heads on a Jimmy Durante look-alike snout. Weevils sometimes are called snout beetles because of their proboscises.

Undoubtedly the most recognizable of the insect proboscises belong to the Lepidoptera. Adult butterflies and moths have coiled tubes that are used to procure nectar and water. These are siphoning mouthparts and are similar in structure and appearance to the party blowouts so popular at New Year's celebrations. The insects use their siphoning proboscises like soda straws to sip nectar from a flower.

The extended mouthparts of some butterflies and moths are as long as the body of the insect. Such super nectar sippers allow insects to get the last drop of nectar from the deepest recesses of flowers. In fact, some flowers depend on these insects for pollination, and Charles Darwin once predicted that an insect possessing a 5-inch proboscis had to exist because he had discovered a flower where a tube that long was needed to extract the nectar. Many years later a moth with just such a proboscis was discovered.

Proboscises in both humans and insects vary widely. One thing is clear, however. Insects, unlike many humans, do not go around sticking their proboscises in other peoples' business!

Insect Eggs

Insect lives are frequently described in terms of a cycle: egg to larva to pupa to adult and back to egg. So the age-old paradox frequently asked of our fine feathered friend, the chicken, might also be relevant to insects. Which came first: the adult or the egg?

Every insect begins life as an egg. Most insect eggs are laid by the adult before the embryo is fully developed. Therefore, the egg doesn't hatch immediately.

Hatching time is usually short, normally within a few days. Since insects don't incubate their eggs, hatching time is determined by the environmental temperature. For instance, the eggs of the Oriental fruit moth will hatch in three to six days in warm weather, but may take up to forty days in cooler weather.

Some insects hibernate in the egg stage. In this case, the egg may not hatch for six to ten months. Grasshoppers and corn rootworms are such insects. The eggs such of the walking stick may remain unhatched for two years.

Fertilization is generally necessary to produce an insect egg that will hatch. Some insect females have, however, eliminated the middleman in the reproductive process. Insects that lay unfertilized eggs include some bees, ants, social wasps, and many aphids. In the social insects, unfertilized eggs develop into males while fertilized eggs become females.

Insect eggs come in various shapes. Some are flat and scalelike. Eggs

of the European corn borer look like fish scales, half covering each other on the leaf of the corn. Others look like miniature wine barrels placed neatly on a dock waiting export. Some of the stinkbugs follow this pattern of egg placement.

The shell of the insect egg can be perfectly smooth. However, some insect eggs are sculptured in striking markings that are the envy of human artists. Generally, the thickness of the shell of the insect egg gives a hint of the environmental conditions it must face. Eggs that hatch shortly after they are laid have thin shells. Eggs that must endure the winter tend to have thick shells. An exception is when the egg is laid in some protected place, such as in the soil or under the bark of a tree.

Some insects cover the egg mass with special materials. Many moths cover the egg mass with hair from their bodies. The female bagworm deposits eggs in the bag which served as her home. The praying mantid secretes a brown, frothlike substance in which to enclose her eggs and attaches the mass to a twig or wire fence, where it remains for the winter.

While it is not possible to answer the question of which came first, it is true that the insect egg must survive if there are to be adult insects. Diversity in the shape, size, and placement of eggs suggests that insects don't put all their eggs in the same basket

Insect Mimics

If mimicry is the sincerest form of flattery, then some insects should feel flattered.

Many insects mimic other insects, but the goal is more basic than mere flattery: it is a matter of survival. Mimicry is one of the mechanisms employed by insects to avoid becoming food for other animals.

Insect mimics are always similar in looks, sound, or behavior to an insect that is dangerous to potential predators. Bees, in general, are avoided by insect-eaters of the world, because many bees are armed and dangerous.

Bees and wasps are equipped with an offensive weapon, the stinger. Most bees and wasps, pacifists in their little insect hearts, prefer not to resort to conflict with other animals. Nature has provided bees and wasps with warning signs—an advertising scheme of color patterns that says "I can be dangerous."

Yellow and brown insects with black stripes are commonly insects that can sting. Stinging insects also produce a particular buzz with their wings. This sound is easily remembered by some animals that have been stung.

Some insects that don't possess a stinger, and couldn't sting even if their lives depended on it, have evolved the color patterns and sound of stinging insects. These mimics gain protection from their similarity to the feared bees and wasps. Such insects include moths, beetles, and many flies. To further the charade, these mimics even act like stinging insects by confronting the potential predator with the angry demeanor of a bee. The behavior

normally works. The predator doesn't hang around to find out the truth for fear of paying the consequences if the insect is the real thing.

Other insects avoid becoming a meal by being bad-tasting; however, it is not enough just to be bad-tasting, you have to advertise the fact by wearing recognizable garb. That makes it easy for predators such as birds to remember the distaste. Some good-tasting insects are look-alikes to their bad-tasting cousins. These mimics then gain a measure of protection against predation, because there happens to be a distasteful "model" on their family tree.

In the world of insects, it's not so much what you know, but who you mimic that makes a difference. Could it be that the same applies to the human fashion statement?

Insect Guts Alive with Bugs

The term "bug" is frequently used as a name for several types of living organisms. Many people call insects "bugs." Technically, not all insects are bugs. But some are! Insects of the order Hemiptera can be called bugs. This order includes stink bugs, squash bugs, boxelder bugs, and bed bugs. These terms are known as common names.

Other insect orders also have common names. Insects classified as Coleoptera are called beetles, Lepidoptera include butterflies and moths, and Diptera are known as flies. Calling these insects bugs would be like calling butterflies beetles.

To make things even more confusing, one-celled microorganisms, especially those that cause disease, are also called bugs. At one time or another, all of us have probably caught a "bug" of this type and gotten sick.

So do bugs of the insect type ever get bugs of the microorganism type? The answer is "yes." Microorganisms attack insects just as they do humans. And when this happens, the insects sometimes get sick and die. In fact, insect-attacking microorganisms are used to control undesirable insects. Such use is known as biological control.

Just as most six-legged bugs are not pests, most microorganisms are not disease-related. In fact, most bugs of both types play beneficial roles in the environment in which they live. Take our digestive system, for instance. It is filled with microorganisms. By some estimates a million million bacteria call the intestines of an individual human home.

Scientists don't understand whether all of those bacteria in the human gut are beneficial but one of the most common is. Named *Bifidobacterium longum,* it is one of the first microorganisms to colonize the digestive tract of newborns. It ferments sugars into lactic acid, and researchers say that is a good thing. That's why some people supplement their diet either by eating yogurt or a commercial product containing lactic acid strains of bacteria. These desirable bugs are frequently called probiotics.

Such good bugs are also found in the guts of insects. For instance, termites and cockroaches frequently consume food that is a suboptimal diet. These insects eat a lot of cellulose material frequently from dead plants. The dead plant material provides a lot of fiber but very few nutrients, and the insects' gut enzymes cannot digest such stuff. That's where the microorganisms come in. These microbes can transform the plant compounds into substances that the insect can absorb as food.

Such a relationship between animals and microorganisms is called symbiosis. This means that both creatures benefit. In this case, the microorganism gets a place to live, and the insect gets help in digesting food. This is also the case with humans and the microbes in our guts.

However, as is always the case in nature, a good thing can be thrown out of whack. For instance, humans might take an antibiotic to kill some "bad" bug, which also kills the "good" microorganisms in the gut. So we will try to replenish with a probiotic.

The problem is even worse for some insects that must molt to grow. Take termites, for example. When they shed their exoskeleton, the inside of their foregut and their hind gut is also shed. That process takes with it the contents of both parts of the gut. Since the good microorganisms live in the hind gut, they are eliminated from the termite's body.

A termite will starve to death without the microbe helpers in its gut. So as soon as the termite molts, it has to replenish the friendly bacteria. Termites don't have doctors or drug stores for such things, but where there is the need, there is a way. The termite simply eats some termite manure, called frass, which is sure to have a good dose of the desirable bacteria. I think I'll opt for yogurt!

The only continent on which butterflies are not found is Antarctica. Even Greenland is home to six species of butterflies that live along the edges of its immense glaciers.

Termite Queens Are the Methuselahs of the Insect World

How long do insects live? This is a question frequently asked by people who encounter insects in their lives. The answer is, "It depends!" It depends on a lot of things. Things like type of insect, the specific stage of development, what food is available, and the temperatures of the environment.

Most insects live relatively short lives—partly because they seldom live out their lives. A high percentage of insects don't die a natural death. They are killed by weather, predators, or accidents, like flying into a car or a bug zapper.

But even if an insect manages to die of old age, it generally will not have lived for more than a year. Annual life cycles are common in the insect world. That is primarily due to the cold-blooded nature of insects, which does not allow them to function in cold weather.

So the general rule in nature is that the life of an insect from egg to death takes a year or less. For example, in the fall grasshoppers lay eggs, which remain in the soil over the winter. In the spring, the eggs hatch, and by August the grasshoppers have reached the adult stage. They mate, lay eggs, and then die before winter. The same is true of praying mantids, katydids, and crickets.

Boxelder bugs also live for about a year, but they spend the winter as adults. In the case of that nasty pest, the Japanese beetle, it is the grub that survives the winter, but the total life of the insect is about a year.

Those aquatic insects known as Mayflies, or fishflies, also have an annual life cycle. The Mayfly adult life is the shortest in the insect world. It lives for only a day. But during the one day that they live, Mayflies manage to mate and lay eggs.

For some insects, their total life is less than a year. If the species completes more than one life cycle during the growing season, individual insects have a very short life span. Some aphids can complete a generation in less than two weeks. How do they do that? Well, some aphids give birth to live young without mating. They cut out the need for mating—and the need for males—and time spent in the egg stage.

Some honey bees also have a relatively short life. Males, called drones, only live about six weeks from egg to death. During the summer, workers also have a short life—about nine weeks. However, the workers that live in the colony over the winter will have an adult life of about a year.

Many insects spend more time in the immature stage than in the adult stage. Some white grub larvae live for three years in the soil, others for five years. In these cases, the adults live for about two months.

One of the longest-lived immature insects is the cicada. The immature of the periodical cicada spends 17 years underground feeding on the sap of a tree. Then it emerges and crawls out of its last immature exoskeleton to seek a mate. During its short adult life of about two weeks, it may not even feed. But it does sing and find a mate!

The longest-living adult insects are the social insects—not all of them, but the queens. Honey bee queens can live up to seven years. Some ant queens live several years as well. But the champions of all insects, in length of life, are termite queens. The mound-building termites of Africa can live up to 60 years!

As we all know, women live longer than men. This is even true in the insect world. Move over, Noah, with your 950 years, and Methuselah, with your 995 years. Here comes the queen of termites. She lives 3,600 human years (relatively speaking).

Roaches can live without food for a month, but will only survive a week without water.

Say It with Perfume

It's not easy to find someone with whom to share your life, especially if you are an insect. In fact, most adult insects devote their lives to that most ancient of biological imperatives—finding a mate.

Insects don't have computer dating lists, lonely-hearts clubs, singles bars, or even a six-legged version of a matchmaker to help in the mating game. Each insect is on its own when it comes to this business of love and marriage.

Insects employ a variety of activities to attract potential mates. Some, like crickets and katydids, are crooners. Others, like the fireflies, are specialists in aerial fireworks. Still others say it with perfume. Yes, for many insects a good scent is worth a thousand sweet words.

Insects that use perfume to announce their availability include butterflies and moths. Technically, these velvet-winged suitors use chemicals called pheromones, which are produced in the insect's body. When released into the environment, these odors are irresistible to the opposite sex. Most pheromones are produced by female insects, but in some species the male is the one in the perfumery business.

How does this all work? The female produces the pheromone and releases it into the environment. To make sure that the chemical gets carried toward potential suitors she flaps her wings about. This creates a plume of air that wafts downwind carrying the sweet scent with it. This process is appropriately named "calling"—sort of the insect equivalent of "Hey, good lookin'!"

Males who happen to be downwind at the time will detect the phero-mone—that's why male moths have fuzzy antennae—and follow the trail upwind to the source. At that point, one is to assume he politely introduces himself and says something like, "Nice pair of legs ... pair of legs ... pair of legs."

Pheromones are complex chemicals. For instance, the pheromone produced by the European corn borer is technically termed (z)-9-tetradecen-1-ol formate. But to a corn borer, that chemical probably rivals the world's sweetest perfume.

We humans once had pheromones of our own. Then we became civilized and began taking baths, and the natural pheromones went down the drain. Thinking individuals that we are, we recognized the importance of such odors and adopted a technological solution to the problem. We make our own pheromones and splash them on. We call them perfumes, colognes, aftershaves, and such. To add to the mystique, we give our pheromones fancy, and sometimes seductive, names. And pay high prices to buy them.

Do you suppose that we humans should admit that we adopted an ap-proach to selecting our mates that was originally perfected by insects? Why not? It certainly makes good scents!

Singing and Stinging Insects Can't Hide Their Sex

The general rule in the animal world is that females and males of the same species look different. Sometimes the difference is in size or color. Birds are often examples of color differences between sexes. Differences also might include the presence or absence of horns. This is the case in some deer and sheep.

Scientifically, a different look between males and females of the same species is known as sexual dimorphism. And the differences are—you guessed it—related to reproduction.

To the untrained observer, male and female insects look the same. In some instances, even experts on insects can't tell bug girls from bug boys. Such a determination would involve dissection of the insect to look at the internal workings.

There are obvious differences between the sexes in some insects. Sometimes the difference is most noticeable in behavior. For instance, any adult insect that stings is a female. That's because the stinger is the insect egg-laying device known as an ovipositor.

Bees and wasps are well-known insects with stingers. However, the females don't fly around with their stingers out in the open. So for most people, getting stung by a bee or wasp is the only sure way to know that the insect is a female. To make matters worse, some male wasps, like the cicada killers, actually act like they are trying to sting. This impostor actually goes so far as poking you with the end of his abdomen!

The ovipositors of female grasshoppers, katydids, and crickets are obvious extensions of the abdomen. These ovipositors resemble curved knives, which is how they function, since they are used to cut plant tissue or soil to deposit eggs.

In some insects, males and females look entirely different. One of the most obvious differences has to do with wings. Males have wings and females do not. This is true of some fireflies. There are also some moths where the male is the only sex with wings. It is true of that pest of evergreen trees and shrubs, the bagworm, where the female stays in the bag. The female of the infamous gypsy moth is also wingless.

In some of the large walking sticks that thrive in tropical regions, the males are winged while the females are wingless. In these insects, the females are also much larger, making the males the "Jack Sprats" of the insect world.

Size-wise, praying mantid males are also lightweights compared to their females. So when a praying mantid female decides to devour her mate, the poor male is fighting up a weight class or two.

Many male moths have fuzzy antennae compared to females of the same species. That difference is related to detecting the mating perfumes, or pheromones. released by the female. The chemicals are trapped in the fuzzy antennae of the male and tell him that somewhere upwind is a female looking for a mate.

Male mosquitoes also have fuzzy antennae. In this case, the antennae allow them to pick up the sounds of the wing beat made by female mosquitoes. That is the same sound that we hate to hear. To the male mosquito, it is music to his antennae.

Some of the most obvious sexual differences in the insect world are associated with stag beetles. The males of these beetles have large horn-like projections that are used in battles with other males. Like their mammal namesakes, the males butt and push each other in contests for territory and females.

The male monarch butterfly has a black spot on each hind wing, something that the female lacks. The black spot is a scent gland that produces a chemical attractive to the female of the species.

Male insects are the songsters of the insect world. Sounds of katydids, crickets, grasshoppers, and cicadas are produced by the male to attract their females.

It is not always easy to tell a female insect from a male. But of this we can be sure: if it stings, it is female; if it sings, it is male.

Insect Breathing Not Dependent on Noses

Animals need oxygen to live. Oxygen must get to cells within the animal, a process called respiration. Vertebrates, including cows, hogs, dogs, salamanders, snakes, and humans, use a circulatory system to do the job. Air is taken into the lungs, where the oxygen is transferred to the blood. The blood is pumped around to cells in the animal by the heart. The system works pretty well.

But it is not the only system used by animals to supply oxygen to cells. In fact, the majority of animals don't have lungs and can't use such a system. These animals are the invertebrates. Invertebrates don't have backbones. They also differ from the vertebrates in other important ways, including how they breathe.

Invertebrates, including the insects, get oxygen to their cells through a series of air-filled tubes called tracheae. These tracheae run within a few cell diameters of each cell in the insect body. At that point, the oxygen diffuses from the tracheae to the cell.

That brings us to another difference in the breathing system between humans and insects. We all recognize that our nose and mouth are the openings that allow air to get to our lungs. Insects, in general, use openings called spiracles to do that job. There are a few exceptions, though. Some very small insects can get the oxygen that they need by diffusion through the cuticle; however, most have spiracles.

Spiracles are openings on the sides of insects that resemble portholes on the side of a ship. These openings are located on the thorax and abdomen of the insect. The number of spiracles varies between insects. The maximum number is ten pairs; such a system is called holopneustic (meaning complete breathing) by scientists.

Not all insects have a full complement of spiracles. Some insects, like fly maggots, have only one or two functional pairs of spiracles. These insects are specialized for living in liquids, such as water or fluids of rotting material.

Humans use active ventilation to get air into and out of their lungs. We contract and expand our chest cavity by contracting or relaxing the muscles of our diaphragm. This forces the air out of our lungs or allows air pressure to fill them up.

Insects generally do not utilize active ventilation. They just let the air move in and out of the spiracles passively. They do have muscles that can be used to close the spiracles when necessary to reduce airflow. When insects need additional oxygen in their system, they increase airflow by telescoping the abdomen. This is much like physically forcing air into and out of human lungs by chest compression during CPR.

Because insects don't need to force air into lungs like mammals, they don't have noses. They do have a proboscis, however. Some human noses of rather large size have sometimes been humorously called proboscises. Insects do have proboscises, but they aren't used for breathing. An insect proboscis is just used for eating!

Cold-Blooded Insects

When you hear the words "cold-blooded," what comes to your mind? Someone who gets cold easily? Or someone who is unfeeling, uncaring, or ruthless? Of course, some of you more hip readers may think of Paula Abdul's song "Cold-Hearted Snake." But most of you probably don't think of insects.

Biologically, humans are not cold-blooded creatures. We maintain our body temperature near 98.6 degrees Fahrenheit, winter or summer. But not so for snakes, salamanders, frogs, earthworms, and insects. These animals are part of nature's "cold-blooded" approach to life. Their body temperatures are near that of their environment.

Such a lifestyle does have its disadvantages, but insects manage to cope. Everything happens more quickly in insects as the temperature increases. They move faster, eat faster, and even grow faster. This means that insects complete their life cycles in less time when the temperature is warm than when it is cool.

When temperatures are too low for activity, some insects rely on the sun for help. They sunbathe, soaking up a few rays to increase their body temperature. These insect sunbathers are called baskers. Like human sunbathers, some insect baskers bathe with their backs in the sun. These are called dorsal baskers. Others prefer the rays on their sides—the lateral baskers.

Some other insects increase their body temperature by vibrating their wings. Moths and bees can frequently be seen with their wings quivering in the cool morning air or in autumn. Such activity is akin to warming up an aircraft engine prior to flight. But with the insect, as soon as the body temperature is high enough, it's off into the wild blue yonder.

Honey bees have a sustained flight temperature threshold of about 54 degrees Fahrenheit. When the air temperature drops below 54 degrees, honey bees may not be able to fly. It is for that reason that some honey bees will be found away from the hive during the cool evening hours of spring or fall. These bees leave the hive when temperatures are suitable for flight but are unable to return when temperatures drop below threshold. Such is the risk that a cold-blooded insect takes when flying near flight threshold temperatures.

Of course in human terms, if the insect is really cold-blooded, it won't matter anyway.

Case Makers of the Insect World

We're all familiar with containers called cases. There are cases in which to store things: eyeglass cases and jewelry cases, for instance. Briefcases and suitcases are designed to carry things.

There are cases that cover the pillows on our beds. We buy individually bottled items, such as beer, soft drinks, or even ketchup, in quantities by the case. Our guns and musical instruments are stored and transported in cases.

Most of us have books arranged in bookcases. Stores and museums use cases of all sorts to display and protect items.

Cases are also used by insects to provide protection, generally in the immature stage. Insects that employ such a strategy are called case makers. And if they drag the case around with them, as we do suitcases, they are appropriately called case bearers.

So how do insects acquire their cases? They don't purchase cases at the local outlet store; they make them. Case-making insects produce silk. They use the silk to tie materials together into the form of a tube. The cases are usually cylindrical with just enough room to house the body of the insect.

The immatures of midges, mosquito-like insects, live in water and produce a small silken tube to which particles of sand or plant matter are fastened.

Black flies, those pesky biting flies, also produce a silken case where they form a pupa and turn into the adult fly. Black fly cases are found attached to rocks in swift streams. Sometimes these golden-colored cases are so numerous that the rocks appear to be covered with a golden silk blanket.

Some insects that live in meal and flour also produce tubes. The Indian-meal moth and the Mediterranean flour moth use strands of silk to join particles of meal or flour. This is the silk mass that we sometimes encounter when we open a container of meal or flour that is infested with these insects.

Another home pest makes a case and is appropriately named. The case-making clothes moth spins a case using silk and the fragments of the material upon which it feeds. The moth adds insult to injury by enlarging its case as it grows.

The evergreen tree pests that we know as bagworms are also case makers. The bag is a case. The larvae of the bagworm, which in the adult stage are moths, use pieces of bark, leaves, or needles to construct this protective shelter. In addition to providing a home for the larvae, the bag is also home to the wingless female and the eggs that she leaves behind. That is why it helps to control this insect pest by removing the bags from the trees during the winter and destroying them. You get rid of next year's worms that way.

The lily-leaf caterpillar creates an unusual case by chewing two pieces of leaf material. The two pieces are then fastened together to form a sleeping-bag type of structure in which the larva lives. As it grows, it just cuts two new pieces and sews them together, as a human mother might do to create a new jacket for a growing youngster.

Casemaking has been developed to a high degree by larvae of the caddisflies. These aquatic insects build their homes out of any type of available material. Caddisfly cases are made of small stones, sand, bits of vegetation, and even small snail shells.

Some creative jewelry makers have put the caddisfly casemakers to work creating works of art. The caddisfly larvae are placed in an aquarium with only one kind of building material—say, sand or precious stones. The larvae build their cases. When the cases are abandoned, the jewelers then create jewelry using the insect-made cases.

Wow! Diamond-studded caddisfly-case earrings—there's a fashion item that is sure to raise eyebrows. After all, how many people do you know who own an abandoned insect case as jewelry?

Cows in Australia create a lot of manure. So much manure, in fact, that these manure piles became serious breeding grounds for buffalo flies and were ruining pastures. So what did the Australians do? They imported dung beetles to disperse and bury it! Today, at least 9 of the 55 species have firmly taken hold in the north Australian landscape.

Most Insects Exhibit Poor Parenting Skills

In the animal world, parenting is something that comes naturally. It's in the genes. Mammal mothers, like deer, dogs, sheep, and cows, lick the newborns and nuzzle them into position to nurse. We call it the maternal instinct.

Adult birds brood the eggs and carry food to the hatchlings in the nest. At night, the mother provides the young with warmth and protection.

In the case of predators like foxes, the parents even teach the young to hunt. The same is true of birds. Outside the nest, the adults show fledgling birds the finer points of rustling up a meal. That is what the clucking and scratching of a mother hen with a brood of chicks is all about. The hen is teaching the chicks how to find food.

While parenting comes naturally to most creatures, the two most successful animals on earth aren't good at it. Humans and insects rank up there among the worst parents in the animal world.

Of course, calling humans and insects poor parents is a value judgment. After all, both groups are highly successful animals. But humans seem to have to learn to parent. Otherwise, why would we buy so many books on parenting? Since Dr. Spock pioneered such books, literally hundreds of titles on the subject have appeared on booksellers' shelves around the world.

Insect parenting varies from minimal input to a sophistication that even we highly evolved humans try to emulate. Most insects leave their offspring to fend for themselves, but even these try to give their kids a good start in life.

The simplest approach to the insect version of child rearing is to do nothing. Some insects simply drop eggs as they feed. Such is the case with some walking sticks, which drop their eggs from the trees. Some cockroaches deposit their egg cases, called ootheca, as they run along. Mayflies actually lay eggs as they die, wherever that may be.

A common insect approach to bringing up junior is to place the eggs in a desirable location. That generally means in a place where the newly hatched insect will find food. For instance, many butterflies and moths will fly around looking for a suitable food plant for their offspring. When the female finds such a plant, she will lay an egg. When the egg hatches, the caterpillar doesn't have to move far to find food.

Sometimes the egg is just placed among food items. Ladybug mothers-to-be deposit their eggs close to aphids. Since ladybugs and their immatures feed on aphids, the baby ladybug is normally surrounded by potential meals.

Many flies feed on dead or decaying plant and animal matter, so the eggs are laid on—you guessed it—dead stuff. That explains why you see flies buzzing around road kill; many are laying eggs. The resulting maggots begin feeding on the rotten flesh.

Insects' placing the eggs in a desirable location would be equivalent to humans' leaving their children in a fast-food restaurant. The food would be there; the kids would have to find it.

Some insects provide the kids' food in bulk—enough food to meet the lifetime needs of the immature. The mud dauber wasps that provision the nest with spiders or caterpillars use this approach. Enough of the prey items are placed in each cell to feed the larvae. Cicada-killer wasps provide a single cicada for each wasp larva. Leaf cutter bees and carpenter bees store enough pollen in a nursery cell to meet the needs of each baby. This would be like a human parent giving a lifetime certificate for the fast-food restaurant.

Some insects, like the paper wasps, supply food as the offspring need it. They are called "progressive provisioning insects" and could be compared to humans who provided coupons for food as needed.

Some insects actually turn over the whole process of feeding the offspring to workers specialized in child care. This is the way of life for social insects, such as ants, termites, bees, and wasps. In this case, the workers prepare the food and feed the kids. Sounds very much like a family that hires a nanny to care for the kids, doesn't it?

Do Insects Have Personalities?

In 1924 Royal Dixon and Brayton Eddy published a book entitled *Personality of Insects.* This delightful book is designed, according to the authors, to present insects to a public that generally lacks knowledge of these creatures.

The book is about the interesting lives of insects, such as how they make music and produce perfumes and light. It compares insect activities to human professions such as agriculturalists, engineers, aviators, and miners. Governance is a topic. But personality, as an attribute of individuals, is not addressed in the book.

To be sure, certain groups of insects, like certain groups of humans, tend to behave in more or less predictable ways. According to the authors, those groups have personalities. But stereotyping insects is as dangerous as stereotyping humans. In insects and in humans, there are exceptions to the rule.

For example, most people would say that bees sting. It is true that many bees do sting. But not all. A few species of bees don't sting because they can't. These are appropriately called stingless bees. There are some species of bees that can sting, but they don't sting humans.

Even within species of bees that sting, not all individuals are able to do so. It is a sex thing. Male bees called drones can't sting. And for a very good reason. Male bees don't have stingers. That's because bee stingers are modified egg-laying devices called ovipositors, which are part of the anatomy of a female bee. When it comes to stinging, male bees just don't have what it takes!

So Dixon and Eddy would be inclined to conclude that the personality of bees is surly. Right down to their menacing buzz. On the other hand, butterflies are delicate and fragile insects that leisurely fly over field and meadow in search of sips of nectar. That is a warm and fuzzy personality, for sure.

The real question is, "Do individual insects have distinct personalities compared to others of their species?" Anyone who has been around animals other than insects knows that individual animals do have personalities. Dog owners know that every dog is not cut out to be a lap dog or a guard dog. Cat fanciers also recognize the differences in personalities from animal to animal. That is why individuals might consider cloning a favorite pet in order to have an animal with the same personality.

Apparently the same thing is true of insects. For instance, we are all aware of the well-publicized difference in stinging behavior between Africanized and other lines of honey bees. Bee keepers have always known that different hives of honey bees have different personalities when it comes to stinging behavior. Some hives are just meaner than other hives and are more easily disturbed. My old bee-keeping neighbor would always warn about making sure to cover up when working a particular hive because, in his words, they were mean SOBs.

People who keep insects or other arthropods as pets have also come to recognize differences in personalities in individual animals. Tarantulas vary widely in how gentle they are and how easily they can be handled. Over the years, kids who have made pets of praying mantids have also recognized that individual mantids behave differently. Some mantids seem to actually enjoy being handled by humans, or at least tolerate it, while others are always trying to escape.

The same is true of the Madagascar hissing cockroaches, which some folks keep as pets. Some Madagascar cockroaches will always produce the namesake hissing sound when handled. Others seem to be less likely to put on such a show. The difference is probably that of type A and type B personality. I'm just guessing. I don't know of any way to accurately assess the personality of a cockroach. Some would say, "Who cares?"

Bees must collect the nectar from two thousand flowers to make one tablespoonful of honey.

Insect Odors Worth a Thousand Words

Insects communicate in a variety of ways. To be sure, insects don't read and write as many humans do. But insects are able to get their message across anyway.

Some insects produce sound for the purpose of communication. Humans have long admired the acoustical abilities of insects. Even poets are moved to pen a few lines to sound-producing insects like crickets, katydids, and cicadas.

A few insects use light to send a message. Almost everyone has seen or heard of the insects called fireflies or lightningbugs. These beetles use a series of light flashes to communicate with each other.

One of the most common approaches to communication among insects is the use of odor. Odors are used by a variety of animals and plants to send messages. Think about the perfume of flowers or the stench produced by a skunk when disturbed!

So how do insects use odors to communicate? Sometimes the odor is used, like a skunk, to gain protection. The stink bug has a name that reflects its use of a bad odor to discourage would-be predators. Anyone who has picked up a stink bug knows that this insect releases a bad-smelling and -tasting chemical under those circumstances.

Ladybugs do the same thing. When handled, these bright-colored insects release a foul chemical through their leg sockets, as anyone who has captured a ladybug knows. That process is known as reflex bleeding, and, like the stink of the stink bug, helps the insect protect itself.

Insects also use odors to attract mates. The French naturalist Jean-Henri Fabre concluded that a female moth released an odor that is attractive to the opposite sex. The basis for his observation was a female peacock moth that had emerged from a cocoon in his laboratory. Within hours, dozens of male moths were attracted to the cage that contained the female. No matter where Fabre moved the female, the males discovered her.

Since the 1870s, when Fabre made his observations, hundreds of insects have been shown to produce chemicals used to attract the opposite sex. The first identification of one of these mate-attracting insect chemicals was made by a German scientist. Adolph Butenandt made the discovery by grinding up the tips of the abdomen of female silkworm moths and presenting various extracts to male moths. The substance that excited the male moths was a kind of alcohol. Butenandt named the chemical bombykol, after the silkworm moth's Latin name, *Bombyx mori.*

Today, chemicals that cause a response in other members of the same species are called pheromones. The word pheromone is from the Greek "carrier of excitement." It is no accident that a human perfume is called "Pheromone!"

Not all insect pheromones are used to attract mates. Some are used as trail-marking substances by ants. Pheromones are used to maintain the caste system in ants, bees, and termites.

Honey bees use pheromones to induce nestmates to sting animals that disturb their nests. Humans can smell this honey bee pheromone. Seasoned beekeepers know that a whiff of this chemical means the bees are getting mad.

A pheromone is designed to send a message to members of the same species. But in the case of the honey bee alarm pheromone, its presence also sends a two-word message to beekeepers: get out!

Insect Ghosts Are Discarded Exoskeletons

Most people call them cicada shells. A byproduct of the massive emergence of the well-known Brood X periodical cicadas is their shells. All cicadas, not just the periodical type, leave shells behind. But cicada shells are not technically shells.

Shells are the hard rigid covering of an animal or an egg. The "animal" part does describe the cicada shells. But scientists generally use the term "shell" for mollusks. That's why creatures like the oyster are called shellfish. Of course, the oyster is not a fish. But that's another issue.

The shells are all that remain of exoskeletons of immature cicadas. The immature cicada that emerges from the soil finds a convenient place to hang. Then, the insect's exoskeleton splits down the back and out crawls an adult. The shell is left behind, discarded like some out-of-fashion item of clothing or a wrapper on a fast-food hamburger.

The portion of the exoskeleton that remains is called an exuviae. The term is used for cast skins, shells, or coverings of animals. The shed skin of a snake is a good example. So in the case of cicadas, what we have is a cast exoskeleton. Some writers call insect exuviae ghosts.

"Ghost" is a good term for what remains of an insect exoskeleton. Frequently, the shed exoskeleton is a shriveled, light-colored, somewhat transparent mass that sort of resembles its original wearer. Ghosts, after all, are rather shadowy figures that retain some attributes of the original creature.

Insect ghosts sometimes are used by entomologists as indicators of past populations of insects. This is especially true of insects known as aphids.

These plant pests multiply very rapidly and leave behind lots of cast skins as evidence of their presence, even if the insects are no longer present.

Shedding and growing new exoskeletons is essential for insects and other arthropods. All creatures that have exoskeletons must shed them as they grow, a process known as molting. As insects grow after hatching, they go through several molts during their immature stages. Each time, they shed their old exoskeleton and grow a new, larger one.

The final molt occurs when the insect goes from the immature to the adult stage. For example, immature dragonflies and Mayflies crawl from the water up the stalk of a plant. There, the adult emerges leaving the exuviae attached to the stem. Mosquitoes crawl out of their pupal skin as they float on the surface of the water.

It is the same process with the cicadas. In this case, the immature crawls from the soil and up a tree or a post. It hangs facing upward while the adult, soft and white in color, crawls from the slit in the back of the old shell. The process normally occurs at night, since the newly emerged insect is soft and cannot fly and is vulnerable to predators. So the cicada uses the protection of darkness to firm the exoskeleton and the wings. By the time daylight comes, the cicada is able to fly.

But the exuviae remain attached to the post or tree. There the shells can be collected by children to use as toys. And what person hasn't, at some time or another, encountered a periodical cicada shell hanging on a tree and marveled at the complexity of nature? Seventeen years underground. No wonder they make so much noise when they emerge!

Great Pretenders of the Insect World

During the 1950s, The Platters had a hit song called "The Great Pretender." The Platters' song was about a human who pretended "that I'm doing well." While humans are good at pretending, insects are among the many animals that are truly the greatest of pretenders.

In the insect world, pretending often is a matter of life or death. To many insects, pretending to be something they are not is a way to avoid becoming a meal for some insect eater.

Some insects pretend to be dangerous—for instance, a fly that looks, behaves, and even sounds like a bee. Most creatures, including humans, have learned that bees and wasps can sting. Consequently, encounters with bees and wasps are avoided when possible. Bee pretenders are shunned by other animals as surely as if they were bees.

Other insect pretenders just look like something that insect eaters wouldn't consider a meal. Sticks and leaves are such things. Plant parts are the food for many animals, including nearly half of all insect species on the earth. But creatures that are predators turn up their noses or antennae when it comes to a vegetarian diet. So looking like a plant part is a good way to avoid encounters with carnivores.

Several groups of insects pretend to be plant parts. Katydids, for instance, have a look that resembles leaves. So when katydids feed in trees, as they do, they blend in nicely. Some grasshoppers use a similar approach to pretending. But many grasshoppers feed on grass plants, so their look is more like grass leaves.

Some treehoppers have shapes that make the insect resemble a thorn. So when these insects are resting, their presence turns a smooth branch into one with thorns. And, as a result, any insect predator moves on in search of its next meal.

Probably the greatest of the insect pretenders are the stick insects. This group of insects gets its common name from its resemblance to sticks or leaves. In temperate regions, most of us are familiar with the walking sticks. Walking sticks are wingless insects that feed in trees. Their long, narrow body shape and the texture of the exoskeleton make them look like small sticks.

The behavior of the stick insects further enhances their great pretense. When at rest, they remain motionless. The walking sticks also extend their antennae and front legs forward to improve the illusion. The walking sticks that live in temperate regions all lack wings, which makes them look even more like sticks.

In tropical regions, the stick insects exhibit more diversity than they do in North America. The greatest diversity is reached in the Oriental tropics, where some stick insects look like walking leaves. Others are quite brightly colored so that they resemble flowers. The walking sticks of the tropics are also larger than those encountered in North America. In fact, some are so much thicker-bodied that they probably should be called walking limbs!

Whether the stick insects look like leaves, twigs, limbs, or flowers, they are the great pretenders of the insect world. And for good reason. For these insects, pretending to be a vegetable is a good way to avoid the attention of a meat-eating carnivore.

Take a Trip to a Zoo of Insects

Many insects are known by common names that may be based on behavior or refer to some obvious characteristic of the insect. Some of these names are suggestive of other animals—animals that are common in zoos.

There are insects called water scorpions. They are among a group of insects that live in water but must come to the surface for air. Water scorpions possess an appendage at the rear that functions as a tube through which air is drawn. They are also predators and catch their prey with grasping front legs. Grasping front legs and a rear appendage are characteristics of real scorpions, thus the name.

The scorpion fly gets its name because of its abdomen resembles that of a scorpion. It actually curls the tip of its abdomen over its back, but unlike its namesake, the scorpion fly can't sting!

There are also lions and tigers in the insect world, including a group of moths known as tiger moths. These moths get their name because many have stripes and are sometimes orange colored like real tigers. And there is the tiger swallowtail butterfly, which just happens to be yellow and black striped.

The tiger also lends its name to a group of beetles. The tiger beetles are vicious predators. They run down their prey and tear it to shreds, sort of like real tigers.

Insect lions include the aphid lion and the ant lion. These insects are of the order Neuroptera and are named after the predatory lion because the immatures of both feed on other insects as predators.

There are even insect pachyderms, elephants, and rhinoceros. Not surprisingly, these insects include some of the largest in North America and the world. Elephant beetle males don't have horns on their heads, but they do have horn-like structures from a structure behind the head. Rhinoceros beetle males have a single horn that protrudes upright from the head, just like a real rhino.

Some insects have bird names. Swallowtails are well-known birds and butterflies. The butterfly gets its name from the long extension from the hind wing that is swallowlike. One is called the zebra swallowtail because it is black with white stripes. Hawk moths get their names because they have long narrow wings and fly very fast. In the grasshopper family is an insect known as the grouse locust, probably because it is mottled brown and blends in with the ground on which it sits.

There are all kinds of insects, and many of them remind us of other animals, such as elephants and lions and tigers, oh my!

Insect Ecology

Relative to the most diverse and successful creatures on the earth, the insects, Pulitzer prize-winning writer Annie Dillard states ,"Theirs is the biggest wedge of the pie." Dillard isn't referring to a batch of ants hauling away a portion of Grandma's apple pie at a family picnic but to the numerical dominance of insects on earth.

Biologists are fond of depicting life on earth as a pie chart with slices representing various living forms according to number of species. About 2% of that pie would be microorganisms; 4% would be the vertebrates, including humans; 22 % plants; and 57 % insects. The remaining 15% would be invertebrates other than insects, including such things as earthworms, millipedes, shrimp, crayfish, and spiders. Regardless of how you slice this pie, insects are a dominant life form on earth.

So what would the earth be like if all of the insects suddenly disappeared? First, it would not be quite as pretty as it is now, because there would be no bright and showy flowers. Flowers exist as a way for plants to attract insects. Without flowers many fruits and vegetables would not be produced. That would reduce the amount of food available for the animals that depend on such plant structures for sustenance. Those animals would disappear.

Animals that feed on insects would also disappear. There would be no woodpeckers, flycatchers, or swallows. No bats or nighthawks. No anteaters or shrews. Many other animals are not exclusively insect eaters but will eat insects when the opportunity arises. These animals would find it hard to meet their nutritional requirements without insect meals.

All kinds of dead stuff would start to accumulate without insects around. About 20% of the insect species feed on dead organic matter and as such are important to the nutrient cycle on this our earth. In the absence of insects, many nutrients would be tied up in things like dead trees lying on the forest floor and dead raccoons on the side of the road.

Of course many plants would not have holes chewed in their leaves, stems, or roots if there were no insects around. That is because about half of all insect species are plant feeders that chow down on living vegetable matter. Insects are the greatest consumers of plant material on the earth.

Insects also feed on animal matter and some 30% of insect species consume living animal tissue. Some insects are predators that consume the entire animal. Other insects, such as blood feeders, just extract some part of the animal. Animals of all kinds—including other insects, birds, fish, and mammals—become meals for insects.

Insects are found in almost all land and fresh water habitats. Not so for the salty sea. No insects live in or on the oceans, but their relatives the shrimp and lobsters do. When it comes to the ecology of insects, it could be said they are on the land and in the air and eat almost anything—but they can't stand the cold!

Our Immigrant Insects

Have you ever wondered why the names of many pest insects refer to foreign places?

It sometimes appears that even insects contribute to the U.S. trade deficit. However, foreign insects began invading our shores long before Washington bureaucrats fretted about the balance of trade. Unfortunately, many of these uninvited insects have stayed here.

German and Oriental cockroaches have infested our homes for many years. Now, in some parts of the United States, the Asian roach has moved in. Many gardeners find Japanese beetles munching on their roses during the summer. Wheat farmers have to deal with Hessian flies and Russian aphids. Corn is attacked by the European corn borer, and soybeans, by the Mexican bean beetle. Apple producers battle the European red mite and the Oriental fruit moth.

American elm trees are now rare because of a disease organism carried by the European bark beetle. The Oriental and Mediterranean fruit flies have played havoc with crops in California, and now the African honey bee reached the U.S. from Central America.

All of these insects are named for their native areas. When people began to travel worldwide, insects hitched a ride. The Hessian fly probably came to the United States in straw bedding used by the Hessian troops during the Revolutionary War. Japanese beetles willingly ride airplanes—many

new infestations begin near airports. The Mediterranean fruit fly sneaks into the country concealed in fruit, which is sometimes concealed by travelers.

Some insects that cause problems were actually "imported"—introduced on purpose. For instance, the African honey bee was introduced to Brazil in an attempt to increase honey production. Gypsy moths, a serious pest of trees, were introduced into the United States by a scientist working on silk production.

All introduced insects are not bad. Some beneficial insects have been successfully introduced into the United States. One such insect is the Vedalia ladybird beetle—a predator of a citrus insect pest.

A few insects native to the United States have managed to find their way to other lands. The American bollworm and the Colorado potato beetle are now worrying farmers outside the United States. When it comes to pest insects moving around the world, some might say, "Share and share alike!"

Some Plants Get the Last Laugh on Insects

In the natural world, insects and plants are almost inseparable. Insect and plant relationships mostly deal with food. The benefits are decidedly one-sided: mostly plants provide the food, and the insects do the eating. There are more than 360,000 species of insects that eat plants. This means that more than 25 percent of all named organisms are plant-eating insects.

Among insects, nearly all of the Lepidoptera (the butterflies and moths) and the Orthoptera (the grasshoppers, katydids, and crickets) are plant feeders. In fact, caterpillars and moths are the primary consumers of plant tissue on the earth. These immature insects are real plant-eating machines. There are also a lot of plant-eating beetles and true bugs.

Having all of these plant-chomping insects around means that many of us look at insects as pests. After all, when we grow a plant as a crop or in a lawn or garden, we are not inclined to share the foliage with a hungry insect. Witness all of the insect-killing chemicals and devices available at the local garden shop.

Plant feeding by insects not only antagonizes humans, it's not very good for the plant either. After all, insects can defoliate plants entirely, burrow into the stems, and even cut the plants off at ground level. Consequently, many plants have developed mechanisms to discourage insect feeding, such as bad tastes or poisons.

As is so often the case, we have to take the bad with the good. In the plant-insect relationship, the good is that the plants have developed a little arrangement where the insect helps with the process of pollination.

Insects play an important role in carrying pollen from plant to plant. The wind also does this. Some plants are self-pollinated, but many enlist insects to do the job. But insects don't work for nothing. The plant has to pay a fee for pollen delivery: the plant provides food for the insect in the form of pollen or nectar.

However, the promise of a handout is not enough. In addition, the plant has a sophisticated advertising system to attract the insect—flowers. These flowers are the beacons that attract the insects. When the insect stops for the free food, the plant dusts the insects with pollen. And some of you probably thought that flowers were there just for human enjoyment! In reality, flowers exist for insects.

Sometimes the insect-plant relationship takes a turn for the worse. In some cases, plants turn the tables on insects and start eating them. The Venus's-flytrap, a plant found naturally in the costal areas of the Carolinas, is a well-known insect-eater. It works by having two jaw-like sides of the trap, which shut when an insect crawls inside. Then the crushed insect is digested, and the nutrients absorbed by the plant. The insect carcass is expelled when the trap is reset.

The sundew is another carnivorous plant. This plant grows in bogs and wetlands throughout the United States. Insects get trapped in sticky hairs in leaf surfaces. Pitcher plants also trap insects in the bulbous pitcher-like stems. In both the sundew and pitcher plant, the insect is digested.

There are more than 350 species of plants worldwide that consume insects. Such plants would seem to be making up just a little for all of those plants that get eaten by insects!

Insects Use Clocks to Tell Time

Most animals, including insects, use clocks to time daily and seasonal activities. These clocks are not timepieces like those produced by Timex or Rolex; animal clocks are internal biological clocks.

How biological clocks keep time is not clearly understood. But like early human clocks, they are based on fluctuations in the environment. Sundials captured the daily rotation of the earth on its axis and calendars mark the earth's rotation around the sun.

These rhythms dictate the activity patterns of most living things on earth. Only animals that live in caves or near the ocean floor do not respond to such daily and seasonal environmental fluctuations. Humans have overcome the need for such behavioral changes with artificial light and housing.

However, we still maintain our biological clocks. That is why we wake up before the alarm goes off in the morning and fall asleep in front of the TV at our normal bedtime. It is also the reason why on trips we wake up in the middle of the night according to local time. Our biological time corresponds to the normal wake-up time where we live.

Human biological clocks can be somewhat useful. They will ring in our heads in time for us to get to work, even if the mechanical alarm doesn't sound. But to other animals, accurate biological clocks are a matter of life and death.

Such is the case for insects. Cold-blooded organisms have to be able to predict the onset of winter, or they perish. For many insects, it is a matter of

one lifecycle per summer. These insects emerge from the overwintering stage, which varies among species, during the growing season. They feed, mate, lay eggs, and generally do what is necessary to get back to the wintering form. For insects that complete several lifecycles during the summer, the process is a bit more difficult. These insects have to predict the onset of fall so that individuals are not killed by cold weather before they develop to a stage that can survive the winter.

Insects, like plants, use the amount of sunlight as an indication of approaching winter, a phenomenon called photoperiodism. The insect responds to decreasing hours of sunlight as a reliable predictor of the approach of fall. Thus shorter days will cause yellow jacket and bumble bee nests to stop producing workers and instead produce queens that will mate and overwinter. Some aphids will stop giving birth to live young and will produce eggs. The eggs will then survive the winter and start the population over again the next season.

That famous migrator of the insect world, the monarch butterfly, uses the number of hours of daylight to schedule the southward migration each fall. The adults that emerge late in the summer forgo mating and head south to spend the winter in the mountains of Mexico. Unlike some warm-blooded birds, insects and insect-eating birds can't hang around during unseasonably warm falls. If they do, a killing freeze will be a disaster.

So insects still use a sundial to tell time. Their lives depend on it!

Insect Antifreeze

November is the time to winterize homes, cars, plants, and even doghouses. Surviving winter demands preparation. It means caulking, putting up storm windows and doors, covering winter-sensitive plants with mulch, insulating dog houses, and possibly getting a flu shot.

What about insects? What do they do when Old Man Winter blows his icy breath across the landscape? Well, they also winterize.

Winterizing for an insect is much like the process we go through to winterize a car. We add antifreeze to the car. Insects add antifreeze to themselves. If the liquid in the cooling system of a motor is allowed to freeze, the expansion during the process will break the radiator and hoses. The same is true of the liquid in insects. If it is allowed to freeze, the crystals that form will destroy the cells and tissues of the insect and cause death.

By adding antifreeze to an automobile's cooling system, the freezing point of the liquid is reduced so that freezing doesn't occur. This protects the system from damage.

As winter approaches, some insects use a similar antifreeze approach. In preparation for freezing temperatures, the water content in the insect is reduced. The water is replaced with glycerol, a compound similar to glycol, which is used in antifreeze. The insect's biological system is shut down and is protected from freezing during the cold winter months.

When the days become longer and the temperatures creep upward,

the insect reverses the process. Glycerol is broken down and replaced with water. The insect is ready to resume normal activities.

In her poem "About Caterpillars," Aileen Fisher begins with this stanza:

> What about caterpillars?
> Where do they crawl
> when the stars say, "Frost,"
> and the trees say, "Fall"?

Good question. But the important thing about an insect surviving winter is not where it crawls, but what it does when it gets there. The successful insects winterize with antifreeze.

Birds Really Go for Bug Chow

Animals that feed on insects are known as insectivores. There are many kinds of insectivorous birds. In fact, the *Peterson Field Guide to Eastern Birds* lists 64 families of birds, and 37 of these families contain species that feed on insects. That does not count birds that dine on other arthropods. For example, some ocean birds feed entirely on insect-related crustaceans like shrimp.

Of the birds that make a meal of insects, some feed on insects when they are available but also eat other things, while others feed exclusively on insects. As their names suggest, the flycatchers and gnatcatchers are part of the latter group. The flycatchers include such familiar birds as the kingbirds and the phoebes. These birds sit on a fence or branch from which they sally forth and snap up flying insects. The kingbirds are known to even feed on honey bees and are therefore not the favorite birds of beekeepers.

The goatsuckers, including the whippoorwill and the common nighthawk, use only insect food collected during the nighttime hours. The nighthawk gets its common name from its habit of diving and swooping in search of night-flying insects.

Other birds that depend on insect food include the familiar swallows and swifts. As these birds fly around during the day, they catch small insects. That is the reason swallows fly in front of a tractor that is mowing hay; the mowing operation flushes insects from the vegetation and provides a dining opportunity for the birds.

Vireos, warblers, wrens, and finches also feed on insects, and many are

exclusively insect feeders. Unlike most other insect-eating birds, wrens will also feed on spiders.

Most birds that depend entirely on insect food are summer residents of temperate regions. As winter approaches, their cold-blooded insect food disappears, and these insect feeders are forced to move south, some even to the southern hemisphere, in order to find food. For most of us, the return of swallows and wrens to our lawns and barns is a joy. It is a sure sign that winter is over—but it also signals that the insect food is back!

One totally insectivorous group of birds does spend the winter in North America. Since the insect food of woodpeckers is under the bark of trees, it is there for the taking in summer and winter.

Other birds that eat some insects include kingfishers and humming-birds. Turkeys, grouse, quail, pigeons, and doves also will not turn down a tasty insect snack. Even some of our least favorite birds, the starlings and house sparrows, consume many insects during the summer months. To some gardeners it is nice to know that even the house sparrow has one redeeming characteristic!

It Takes Gall

Almost everyone has, at one time or another, noticed a deformity in plant growth called a gall. These abnormalities can be caused by insects. Gall-causing insects lay their eggs in plant tissue, and the developing larvae cause the plant to respond with abnormal growth. Some beetles, moths, flies, and wasps are among the insect gall-makers.

Galls have been recognized by humankind for centuries; in fact, galls are better known than the insects that produce them. The galls are numerous and showy; their insect residents, on the other hand, are quite small and difficult to see.

From times of old and even today, galls have been used to produce tannic acid and dyes, including one dye called Turkey Red. The best permanent inks have, for years, been produced from galls. The Aleppo gall, found in eastern Europe and western Asia, is used for this purpose. In some places, the law requires that permanent records be made with ink derived from galls. Such an ink is used by the United States Treasury and the Bank of England.

Gall insects attack over one-half of all plant families, and almost all parts of the plant are subject to infestation. In general, gall-makers produce the same type of gall on different plants.

Galls are generally named according to the way they look. For instance, we have the hedgehog gall, which must look a bit like a hedgehog. Many galls remind folks of fruits and vegetables, including the apple, potato, and pea galls of oak. We also find spindle, hairy, and spiney galls on oak. And there

are button galls, cup galls, and the red sea urchin galls. Bullet galls and vase galls have been known to occur on the same plant as the wool-sower galls.

One of the most interesting of the galls is the jumping oak gall. When this gall falls from its oak tree host, the larvae inside cause the gall to jump. The popping activity of the jumping gall is similar to that of Mexican jumping beans, which is also caused by an insect inhabitant.

Even in the insect world, a little gall can sometimes attract attention!

Fleas can jump 30,000 times without stopping, and can leap 150 times their own height. That would be like a six-foot-tall man leaping over three Statues of Liberty stacked on top of each other!

Bugs Know When Spring Has Sprung

Everyone has their favorite indicator that spring has sprung. For some it's the peep of the peeper. This little frog begins singing early in the season and is appropriately called the spring peeper.

Other people turn an eye to the sky and note the flight of migratory waterfowl. Ducks and geese headed north indicate that winter may be winding down. A robin red breast hopping on the lawn in search of an earthworm indicates to some folks that the sound of lawn mowers cannot be far behind.

But sometimes peepers are quieted by a frozen pool, and migrating ducks and geese are forced to land because of a late winter snowstorm. Even the old robin has been seen chirping forlornly from an ice-encrusted branch.

Native Americans turned to the butterfly as a sure indicator of spring. In the southwestern part of the United States, the Zuni tribe held that "When the white butterfly comes, comes also the summer."

Butterflies specifically, and insects in general, aren't as likely as frogs and birds to make a mistake when predicting the end of winter conditions. Even the term "butterfly" shows how confident ancient people were about this insect when it came to the seasons. Butterfly is a short version of "fly of the butter season," or spring. This was because spring was when cattle traditionally gave birth and produced milk and cream, which was used to churn butter.

Insects are unable to function in temperatures below 50° F, so it is important for them to make sure summer is here before they arrive. In general,

insects remain in hibernation until all chance of freezing temperatures is past. However, there are exceptions.

Some insects overwinter in protected places as adults. These insects are some of the first seen in the warm days of late winter or early spring. Such insects as ladybugs and some flies commonly come out of hibernation as temperatures rise and can be seen crawling or flying around our homes. Some of the first insects seen in the early spring are the large overwintering queens of bumble bees and wasps. These queens hide in protected places and emerge in late spring and early summer to begin a new colony.

There are even a couple of butterflies and several moths that overwinter as adults and can be seen flying around on the first warm days. In general, though, butterflies overwinter as pupae and don't show up until summer is safely here to stay.

So if you're trying to predict the end of winter, do as Native Americans have done for centuries. Ignore the birds and frogs, and put your money on the butterflies. After all, they are not called flies of the butter season because they have a habit of getting frost on their wings!

Winds of Winter Not Favorite Thing to Insects

Two of Maria's favorite things in *The Sound of Music* were "snowflakes that stay on my nose and eyelashes and silver white winters that melt into spring." Not so to insects. Everything about winter is a life-and-death matter to many animals, especially insects.

Insects are cold-blooded creatures that generally cannot control their body temperature; therefore, they can't function in winter. As the poet Aileen Fisher once wrote about insects: "None has the least little urge to know what the world is like when the sky says 'snow.'"

So these six-legged creatures have several approaches to surviving winter conditions. A few, like many other animals, move to warmer climates during winter. The monarch butterfly is the best known of the insects that migrate. The monarch prefers the cool, but not freezing, temperatures of the mountains of Mexico to a more northern exposure to winter.

Many insects try to survive winter and fail. These unsuccessful snow bugs include the well-known moth that is a cutworm in the immature stage. Known as the black cutworm, it goes into the winter in many stages, none of which survive. So each spring, the black cutworm population is replenished by migrants from more southern climes.

Many other insect species also die during the winter and ride the winds of spring back into northern areas. Included are some plant pests, such as aphids and leafhoppers. The small green leafhopper that manages to come through our window screens and die in our light fixtures is a summer resident only.

Most of the insects that we encounter each summer do manage to survive the local winters. Some of these insects live in the soil and move deeper as the soil freezes. The white grub that damages our lawns is such an example. It just digs deeper and stays below the frost line. When the spring thaw arrives, it reverses the movement and comes back to the surface.

Many adult insects that don't move south for the winter seek some shelter from the environment. Several species of insects actually take up residence in our homes, much to our concern at times. Ladybugs move in great numbers into protected places during the winter. That protected place is frequently under the bark of a dead tree, under a stone, or in the leaf litter. Sometimes the ladybugs mistake our houses for dead trees or stones and move in with us.

Ladybugs are not the only winter intruders in our homes. We also can find a fly called the cluster fly in great numbers, hibernating in wall spaces and attics. The same is true of some paper wasp queens. These ladybugs, flies, and wasps frequently show up inside our homes, attracted by the warm temperatures within.

Many other insects survive winter in the egg, larval, or pupal stages. Many times the eggs are located in protected sites. For instance, eggs of the corn rootworm are snug in the soil where the female placed them. Eggs of the praying mantid are encased in a foamy covering and attached to a stem, where they will stay until the next spring.

Many overwintering larvae also are located in protected sites. European corn borer caterpillars stay inside the corn stalk until the warmth of spring causes them to go into the pupal stage. Woollybear caterpillars crawl around and find a nice protected place, such as plant trash or even hay in a barn.

Many caterpillars change into pupae as winter approaches. Some hide in the soil; others spin a cocoon and sleep in a silk blanket during the snowy days of winter.

All of these insects are winterized. They produce a natural antifreeze that keeps their cells from freezing when the temperatures drop below 32° F. The chemical is glycerol, which is very similar to the antifreeze materials used in automobiles to keep radiators from freezing.

To insects, the approach of winter means winterize and hibernate. The sign outside a cocoon covered with snow just might read: "Snug as a bug in a rug! See you next spring!"

In Africa swarms of Orthoptera (desert locusts *Schistocerca gregaria*) may contain as many as 28,000,000,000 individuals.

References and Recommended Reading

Bastin, Harold. *Freaks and Marvels of Insect Life.* New York: A. A. Wyn, 1954.

Brallier, Floyd. *Knowing Insects through Stories.* New York: Funk & Wagnalls Company, 1921.

Cheesman, Evelyn. *Everyday Doings of Insects.* NewYork: Robert M. McBride and Company, 1925.

Comstock, Anna Botsford. *Ways of the Six-Footed.* Boston: Ginn & Company, 1903 (reissued Ithaca: Cornell University Press, 1977).

Cornwell, P. B. *The Cockroach.* London: Hutchinson, 1968.

Dixon, Royal, and Brayton Eddy. *Personality of Insects.* New York: Charles W. Clark Co., 1924.

Evans, Howard Ensign. *The Pleasures of Entomology.* Washington: Smithsonian Institution Press, 1985.

Fabre, Jean Henri. *Fabre's Book of Insects.* New York: Dodd, Mead and Company, Inc., 1921.

Harpster, Hilda T. *The Insect World.* New York: The Viking Press, 1947.

Headstrom, Richard. *Adventures with Insects.* New York: Dover Publications, Inc., 1963.

Hocking, Brian. *Six-Legged Science.* Cambridge, Mass.: Schenkman Publishing Co. Inc., 1968.

Howard, L. O. *The Insect Book: A Popular Account of the Bees, Wasps, Ants, Grasshoppers, Flies and Other North American Insects . . .* Garden City, N.Y.:Doubleday, Doran & Co., 1923.

Lauck, Joanne Elizabeth. *The Voice of the Infinite in the Small.* Mill Spring, N.C.: Swan Raven & Co., 1998.

Lutz, Frank E. *A Lot of Insects: Entomology in a Suburban Garden.* Cornwall, N.Y.: The Cornwell Press, Inc., 1941.

Pain, Nesta. *Lesser Worlds.* New York: Coward-McCann, Inc., 1958.

Riley, James Whitcomb. "The Doodlebugs' Charm." *The Works of James Whitcomb Riley,* vol. 8: *Poems Here at Home,* pp. 116–117. New York: Charles Scribner's Sons, 1908.

Sargent, Theodore. *Legion of Night: The Underwing Moths.* Amherst : University of Massachusetts Press, 1976.

Snodgrass, Robert. E. *Insects, Their Ways and Means of Living.* New York: Smithsonian Institution Series, Inc., 1930.

Stokes, Donald W. *A Guide to Observing Insect Lives.* Boston: Little, Brown & Company, 1983.

Sutherland, Harvey. *The Book of Bugs.* New York: Street & Smith, 1902.

Tweedie, Michael. *Insect Life.* London: William Collins Sons & Co. Ltd., 1977.

Thoreau, Henry David. "The Battle of the Ants." In *The Writings of Henry David Thoreau, Journals,* edited by Bradford Torrey, vol. 3, *September 16, 1851–April 30, 1852,* pp. 209–212. Boston: Houghton Mifflin, 1906.

Index